For REASONS of STATE

Angelique Campens
Erica Cooke
Steven Lam

WHITNEY MUSEUM OF AMERICAN ART, NEW YORK
DISTRIBUTED BY YALE UNIVERSITY PRESS, NEW HAVEN AND LONDON

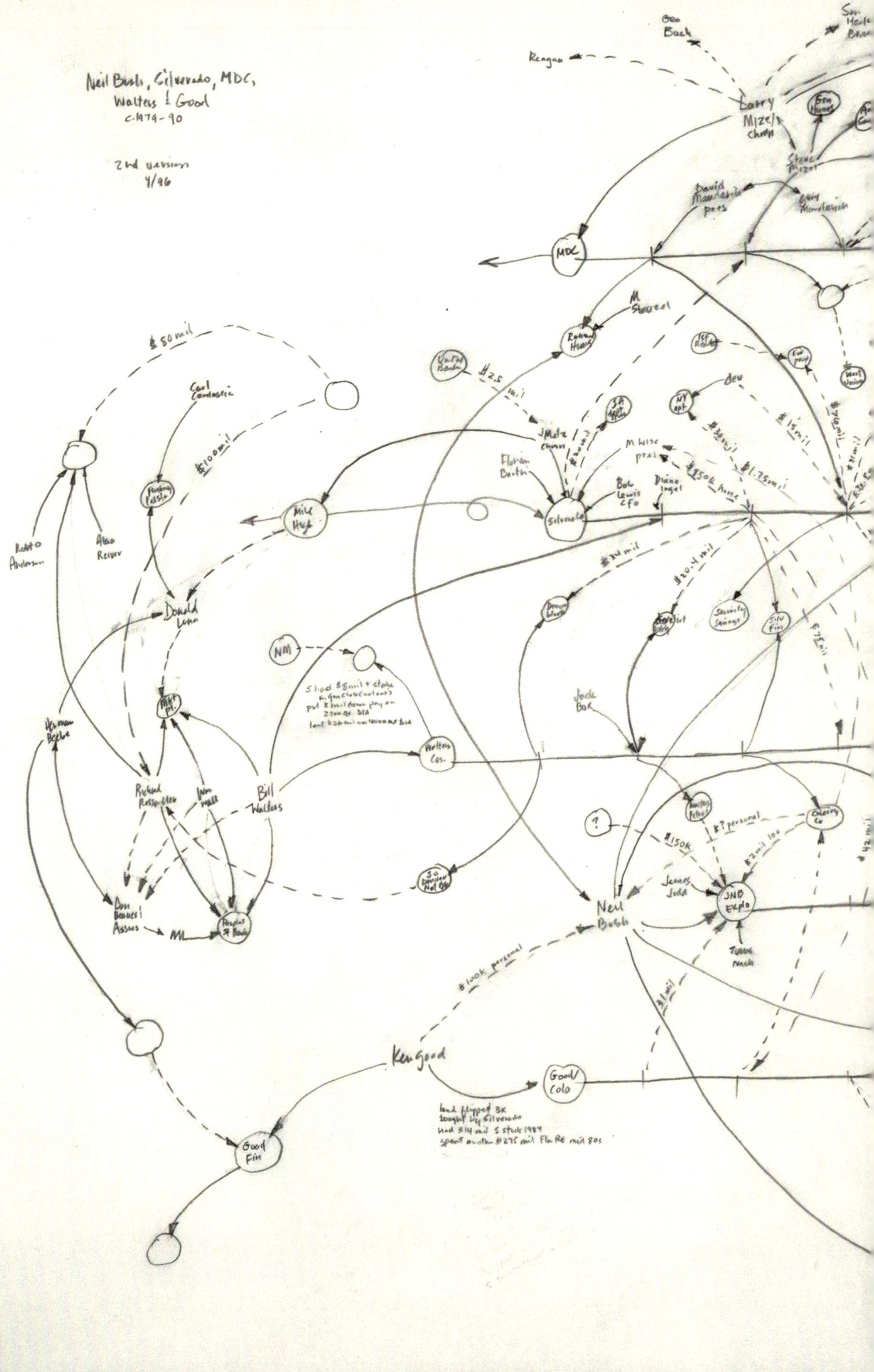
Neil Bush, Silverado, MDC, Walters & Good
c.1979-90
2nd version
4/96
Reagan
Larry Mizel chmn
Steve Mizel
David Mandarich pres
MDC
Richmond Homes
$2.5 mil
J Metz chmn
M Wise pres
Florian Barth
Bob Lewis CFO
Silverado
Mile High
$80 mil
$100 mil
Robt O. Anderson
Alan Reiver
Donald Lunn
NM
Herman Beebe
Richard Rossmiller
Bill Walters
Walters Cos.
$34 mil
$20.4 mil
$15 mil
$1.75 mil
$150K house
NY apt
?
$150K
$? personal
$2 mil loan
James Judd
JNB Explo
Neil Bush
$100K personal
$1 mil
Ken Good
Good/Colo
Good Fin
land flipped 3X
bought by Silverado
had $14 mil S stock 1984
spent another $275 mil Fla RE mid 80s

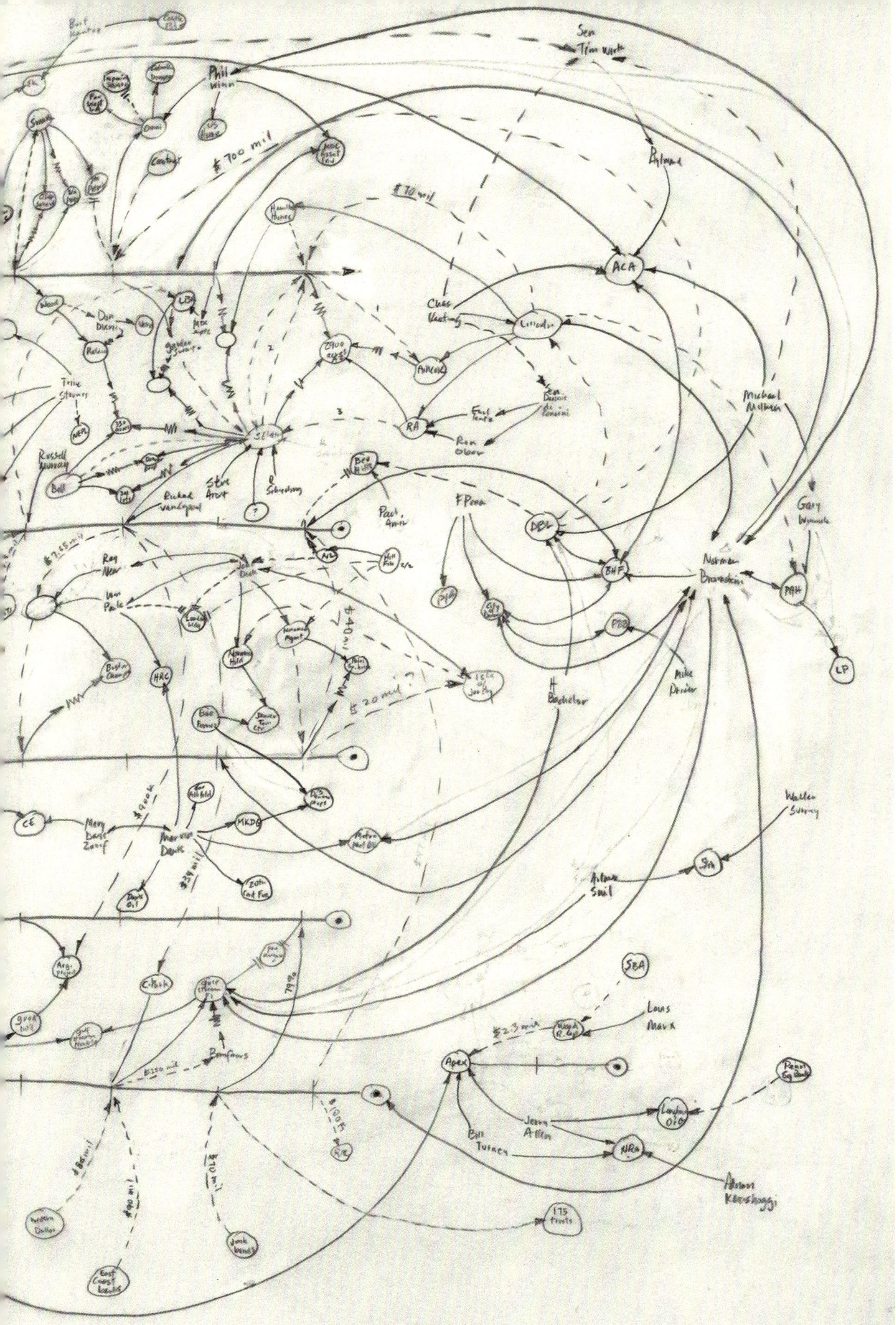

This catalogue was published on the occasion of the exhibition *For Reasons of State*, May 16–June 7, 2008, curated by the 2007–08 Helena Rubinstein Curatorial Fellows of the Whitney Museum of American Art Independent Study Program: Angelique Campens, Erica Cooke, and Steven Lam.

The Independent Study Program is supported in part by Joanne Leonhardt Cassullo, The Dorothea L. Leonhardt Foundation, Inc.; the Dorothea L. Leonhardt Fund of the Communities Foundation of Texas, Inc.; The Edward and Sally Van Lier Fund of the New York Community Trust; the Easton Foundation; and the Whitney Contemporaries of the Whitney Museum of American Art. Endowment support is provided by the Communities Foundation of Texas, Inc.; The Dorothea L. Leonhardt Foundation, Inc.; the Helena Rubinstein Foundation; and George S. Harris.

WHITNEY
Whitney Museum of American Art
945 Madison Avenue
New York, NY 10021
whitney.org

Design: Sarah Vogwill
Printing: Prints Charming, Boothbay, Maine

Set in Interstate and printed on Mohawk Via

ISSN: 1068-7823
ISBN: 978-0-300-14694-3

Yale University Press
302 Temple Street
P.O. Box 209040
New Haven, CT 06520
yalebooks.com

Frontispiece: Mark Lombardi, *Neil Bush, Silverado, MDC* (2nd Version), 1996; contents page: The Bureau of Inverse Technology, still from *Bit Plane*, 1999 (detail); page 40: Bureau of Inverse Technology (Agents Natalie Jeremijenko and Kate Rich) *Anti-terror Line*, 2004–08; page 44: Speculative Archive (Julia Meltzer and David Thorne), still from *"It's not my memory of it": three recollected documents*, 2003

Printed and bound in the United States
10 9 8 7 6 5 4 3 2 1

CONTENTS

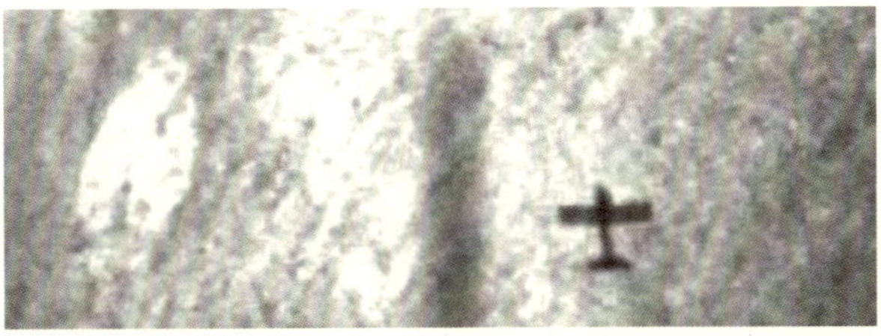

Still from *Secrecy*, 2008. Directed by Peter Galison and Robb Moss.

INTRODUCTION

IN 1589, the Italian political theorist Giovanni Botero defined "reason of state" to be the "knowledge" in which a state "may be founded, preserved, and extended."[1] Through this concept, he insisted that the nation should, first and foremost, preserve its sovereignty, even if the ethical and legal concerns of its citizenry were compromised as a result.

Today, this notion of national interest and preservation of the state has adopted a sinister tone in the United States. When the American government invokes reasons of state, this proposition camouflages illegitimate actions and policies, enabling the government to proceed without appropriate constitutional checks and balances. The Bush administration wiretaps phones for reasons of state. The CIA erases tapes documenting questionable interrogation practices for reasons of state. Telecommunications companies that illegally share customers' information for purposes of national security are often exonerated for reasons of state. Contrary to Botero's definition of "knowledge" as establishing, protecting, and expanding the state, the current use of reasons of state speaks to governmental control of knowledge undermining the credibility of national interest, thereby threatening the state's preservation. While governmental regulation of the open transmission of information may sometimes be justified, the larger questions concerning public access to information—who gets to hear and see what, when, and how—and its value in constructing alternative histories, are often neglected.

Bik van der Pol, the Bureau of Inverse Technology, Jenny Holzer, Lin + Lam, Mark Lombardi, Julia Meltzer and David Thorne, Trevor Paglen, Ben Rubin, and Susan Schuppli reveal information to the public that is otherwise censored or misrepresented due to government or corporate influence. This strategy of counter-information challenges the security claims and property rights that limit public access. Foreshadowing the upcoming presidential election, this exhibition addresses the ability of citizens to function as a democracy in the face of governmental secrecy. Their artworks prompt viewers to reconsider exchanging our current use of the "need-to-know" for a more democratic "right-to-know."

The contributions in this catalogue situate these artworks as sites of critical engagement to explore how secrecy supplants transparency in the current administration. Erica Cooke considers how the works of Lombardi, Paglen, Rubin, and the Bureau of Inverse Technology surveil today's corporate environment in which policies in favor of privatization jeopardize public assets and civilian liberties. Steven Lam examines artworks by Meltzer and Thorne, Lin + Lam, and Schuppli, exposing how these artists counter state secrets through the investigation of official archives. Angelique Campens discusses erasures and disappearances in the aesthetic procedures of Holzer, Rubin, and Bik van der Pol. Also included is an interview with Peter Galison and Robb Moss, codirectors of the 2008 documentary *Secrecy*, which further complicates the question of whether secrecy will save or corrupt our future well-being.

1. Giovani Botero, *Reason of State*, trans. P. J. Waley and D. P. Waley (New Haven: Yale University Press, 1956), 3. Botero's "reason of state" has evolved into the phrase "reasons of state" that is more commonly used today.

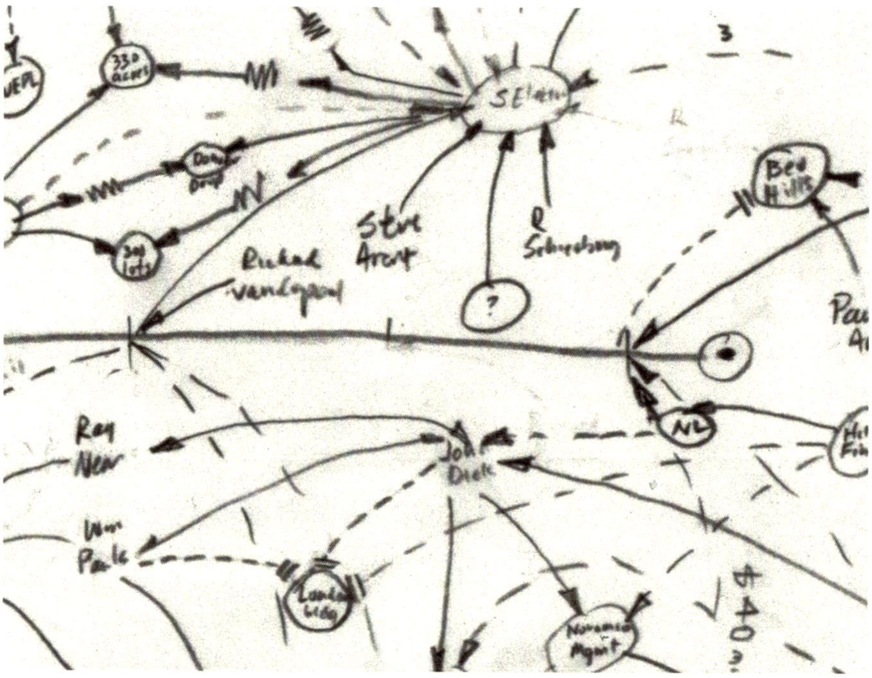

Mark Lombardi, *Neil Bush, Silverado, MDC* (2nd version), 1996 (detail)

STRICKEN FROM THE RECORD: THE PUBLIC'S ACCESS TO GOVERNMENTAL PRIVATIZATION

Erica Cooke

AMERICA'S INCREASING capitalist appetite for possession of and profit from any person, place, or thing is at the core of today's reigning neoliberal ideologies. Prior to becoming common practice in the 1980s, neoliberalism existed as a marginal theory following the 1947 creation of the Mont Pelerin Society, a group of influential thinkers, including University of Chicago economist Milton Friedman, his predecessor Frederick von Hayek, and, for a considerable amount of time, Karl Popper. Through privileging private property rights, a free market, and free trade, these economic theorists promoted capital accumulation and repudiated the benefits of an interventionist state—the very premise of Keynesian economics that dominated U.S. policy after World War II. Neoliberalists seemed to disappear from political visibility over the decades following the war, but in actuality they were quietly consolidating the support of corporations, powerful individuals, and newly formed international institutions such as the World Bank, the World Trade Organization, and the International Monetary Fund.

At the first sign of a faltering economy in the 1970s, neoliberalism quickly presented itself as an alternative to Keynesian politics under the premise that classical liberalism and Adam Smith's notion of the invisible hand of the market[1] would guarantee economic stability. Neoliberalism continues to convince a majority of voters that free-market policies will grant everyone equal access to ownership, control, and competition in the market, even when disregard of social responsibility is plainly visible.[2] Journalist Naomi Klein, for example, theorizes that today's neoliberals, disciples of Friedman, seize and manipulate moments of collective trauma (natural disasters, war, and disease) to reap the benefits of communal loss: "Some people stockpile canned goods and water in preparation for major disasters; Friedmanites stockpile free-market ideas."[3]

Current legislative strategies of the government, such as contracting commercial institutions to provide military and technological services and expanding national security programs through telecommunications companies, reflect what can be considered the creation of a fourth branch of government that was formed without taxpayers' consent and is unaccountable to its citizenry. This process, known as privatization, transfers state-run entities to the private sector, opening up new terrain for profitable activity. The appeal of privatization is that governments can act through corporations (and vice versa), which removes transparency of who authors and implements often contentious regulations that relinquish social obligations.[4] These increasingly covert exchanges between the state and corporations sever the direct tie between power and responsibility, making it more and more impossible to locate sources of power.

According to political theorist Hannah Arendt, "While strength is the natural quality of an individual seen in isolation, power springs up between men when they act together and vanishes the moment they disperse."[5] Power is the force connecting those within the corporation to each other as well as to political and economic allies; it is the access to knowledge that these particular affiliations afford. While U.S. law grants the corporate body equal status as civilians, corporate power far surpasses that of an ordinary citizen.[6] Corporate influence over what knowledge the state deems necessary to disclose to the public is evidence of how civil liberties, especially our "need to know," suffer in exchange for commercial interests.[7] Artists Mark Lombardi, Trevor Paglen, Ben Rubin, and the Bureau of Inverse Technology attempt to counter this culture of privatization, and resulting secrecy, by envisioning often invisible information. Their shared method of compulsively gathering information aims to reveal hidden connections suggestive of government and corporate malfeasance. The resulting presentations of such information, at once granted and barred, align the public's denied access to knowledge with the neoliberal reconfiguration of ownership and wealth over the past thirty years.

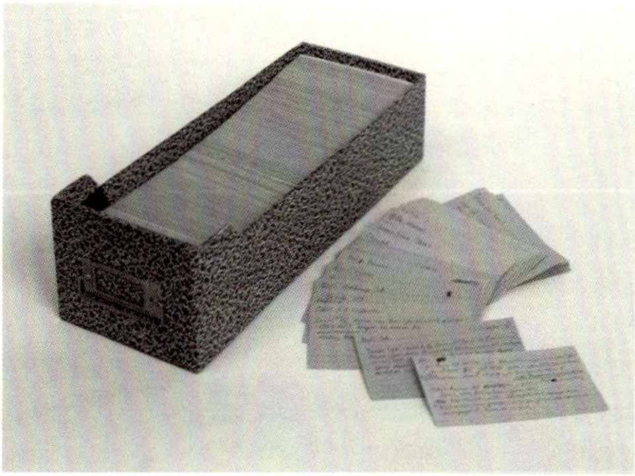

Mark Lombardi's collection of twelve thousand index cards is used as an archival reference for the people, corporations, and government agencies implicated in his drawings.

From 1994 until his death in 2000, Lombardi produced flowcharts of major economic-political scandals from the mid-1970s through the early 1990s, which he referred to as "narrative structures." To draft these diagrams, Lombardi would execute successive versions of each flow chart, often making more than ten.[8] As a second version that did not undergo further revisions, *Neil Bush, Silverado, MDC*, is a relatively small, delirious, and incomplete map of lines connecting to circles that name people and companies involved in the 1980s U.S. savings and loans scandal. The deregulatory policies of Ronald Reagan provided the savings and loan industry more autonomy than they merited given their severely endangered financial status.

In fact, the Reagan administration was recognized for its wide-scale implementation of neoliberal policies—reducing social programs, cutting taxes to promote industry, facilitating the movement of financial powers, and more—as influenced by Paul Volcker, chair of the Federal Reserve, and Milton Friedman. With leeway to act as banks without regulatory restrictions, these ever-inventive institutions engaged in one of the largest money laundering schemes in history, costing taxpayers five hundred billion dollars over thirty years.[9] Following on the heels of journalist Pete Brewton's book *The Mafia, CIA and George Bush: The Untold Story of America's Greatest Financial Disaster*, Lombardi's work is especially sensitive to the "layers of protection and insulation" surrounding the bi-partisan scandal that made it impossible to track "money from the saving and loans to its ultimate destination."[10] This inability to link origins with outcomes —a means of facilitating neoliberal policy—is a perfect metaphor for Lombardi's case study of money laundering and its intricate web of organized crime figures, intelligence agencies, and corporate intrigue.

Whereas traditional flowcharts express a transparent lineage of information, Lombardi subverts this common business format to unveil a closed circuit of power in the savings and loan industry. This closed circuit of concentrated wealth

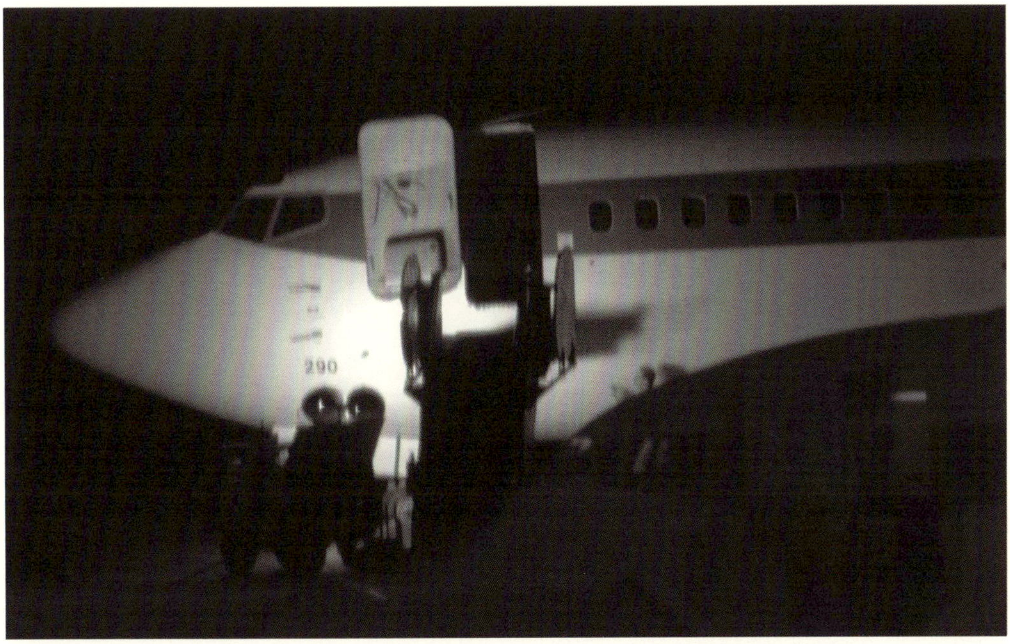

Trevor Paglen, *Unmarked 737 at 'Gold Coast' Terminal/Las Vegas, NV/Distance ~1 mile/10:44 pm*, 2005

clearly illustrates that the personal gains of a few did not occur by accident but because of premeditated efforts encoded in policies that put the common good at risk.[11] Lombardi draws on paper with graphite to produce a sketchbook surface marred with traces of erased marks. This medium allows Lombardi to remove and redraft marks in response to the circumstantial evidence surrounding the failed Silverado savings and loans scandal and its list of participants, such as CIA agents and a board of directors that included George H. W. Bush. Although Lombardi invented a line legend for his "narrative structures," it only appears in secondary materials about his work, and observers are left to follow their own intuition in identifying the various types of relationships. As defined by Lombardi, a dotted line, for example, represents a "blocked or incomplete transaction," a line with double arrows indicates "some type of mutual relationship or association," and a line with one arrow is "some type of influence or control."[12] With or without the legend, the immense array of lines and circles reads as an unfolding, not only of a major financial calamity, but also of the mental pressure placed on a fervent researcher to make nearly impenetrable data perceptible and accurate.

Lombardi had a database of more than twelve thousand handwritten index cards that he integrated into the preliminary research for his drawings. According to curator Robert Hobbs, he "would often lay them directly on the paper and shuffle them around as he worked."[13] This rigor to visualize the exchange—to create "a visible aesthetics for the invisible net"—has its history in the 1960s when architect Buckminster Fuller and theorist Marshal McLuhan had labored over perfecting the triangulated space frame that could "make poetic images of the invisible communication infrastructure whose influence

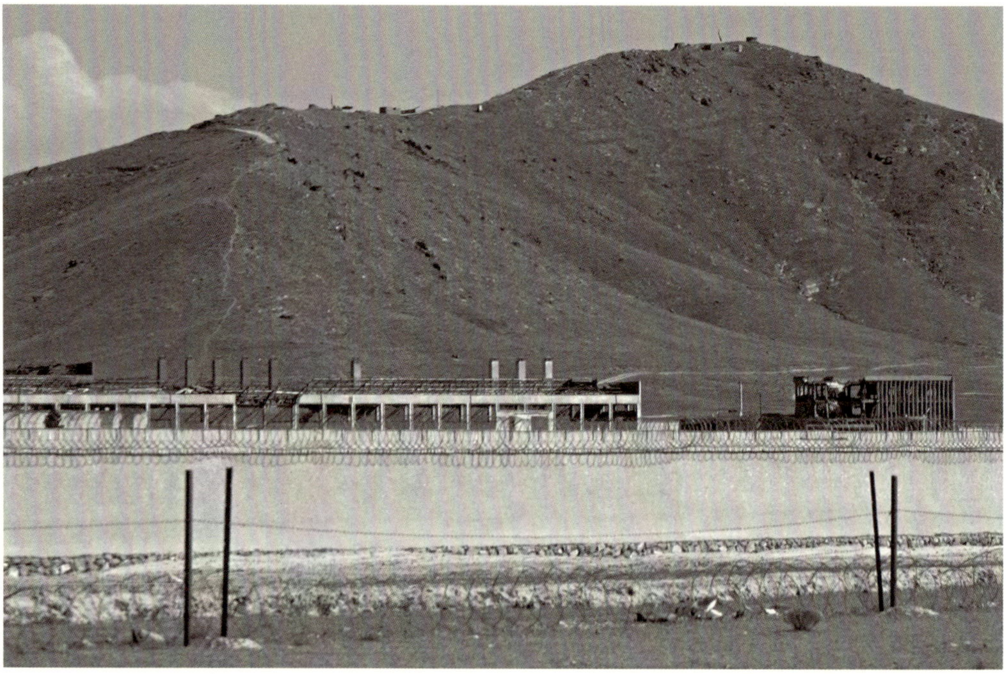

Trevor Paglen, *The Salt Pit, Northeast of Kabul, Afghanistan*, 2006

had grown throughout the century."[14] While Lombardi's weblike structures did inherit the physical structure of a network implied by Fuller and McLuhan's models, Lombardi did not believe that these structures could be sites of potential interconnectivity.

Neil Bush, Silverado, MDC is rife with visual uncertainty, and despite implications of being called a "narrative structure," Lombardi complicates our reading of the scandal with lines that point to circles without names, sweeping arcs that lead to empty areas outside of the diagram, and five horizontal lines that divide the space for no apparent reason. Even definitive connections are questionable given how the CIA often operates through "a frontman or middleman set up to protect the identities of the primary participants," who "may or may not know for whom he is working and the actual purpose of his work."[15] These misidentified figures and missing information make the process of labeling and tracing routes nearly impossible. The surface reading of labels, lines, and circles, coupled with missing and misleading information, further exacerbates the viewer's struggle to gain any specific details within given relationships.

Whereas Lombardi's chart intensifies the secrecy of power by illustrating the chaos of form as well as the unknown or mistaken identities of people involved, Trevor Paglen's photographs of prison camps, military bases, and planes suggest how power can be hidden in plain sight. "Extraordinary rendition" refers to the American government's program of kidnapping and transporting suspected terrorists around the world to places where torture is more routine. To enable the government to execute extraordinary rendition, which includes persecution beyond Geneva

Convention limits and surveillance of citizens without warrant, there needs to be a "legal form of what cannot have legal form," or what Giorgio Agamben called a "state of exception."[16] Agamben claims that "recurrent opinion posits the concept of necessity as the foundation of the state of exception," whereby "'necessity has no law'" can be "interpreted in two opposing ways: 'necessity does not recognize any law' and 'necessity creates its own law.'"[17] President George W. Bush and his administration abuse this concept of necessity to justify reinterpreting legislation that limits their power, supporting the fabrication of new legislation that enhances their sovereignty.[18]

Endorsed by infrastructure contractors like Halliburton, the CIA has and continues to form a network of secret "black sites," which can be defined as the military and prison industrial complexes used to detain and relocate prisoners. Paglen's fixation on the landscape of the black world—an appropriate metaphor for a world mired in covert operations and cover-ups—extends to his tracking the underground movement between black sites and U.S. military bases. *Unmarked 737 at 'Gold Coast' Terminal/Las Vegas, NV/Distance ~1 mile/10:44pm* (2005) is one among a series of photographs that Paglen took of unmarked civilian planes believed to be involved in the intricate system of transporting prisoners from one point to another. The plane in the photograph bears no military markings nor shares any likeness to military vehicles because it is most likely owned, as the photo suggests, by a subsidiary of Boeing, such as Jeppesen Dataplan. While the cloak of corporate identity enables the CIA to maneuver within foreign airspaces otherwise restricted to the U.S. government, this strategy decreases government accountability, warping a concern of national security into a profit-driven enterprise.

The governmental decision of where and on what terms to outsource military defense debunks the neoliberal notion of smaller government being essential to, or even harmonious with, a free-market economy. The government can therefore maintain a powerful—albeit less noticeable—political and economic presence. Black sites, a phenomenon of the Bush administration, are closely associated with allegations of prisoner maltreatment as well as the corporate body whose specialization and aid has made this network possible. Akin to Lombardi's research-based approach to the U.S. savings and loans scandal, Paglen culls together all available public resources (including a map from a former prisoner, commercial satellite imagery, and testimonies of informed Afghani citizens) to find the "Salt Pit," an abandoned brick factory northeast of Kabul that had been transformed into the largest CIA-run interrogation facility and prison in Afghanistan. Despite the abnormal activities that occur within this facility, Paglen's *The Salt Pit, Northeast of Kabul, Afghanistan* of 2006 is a banal image of the factory's exterior and its environs, almost rendered lifeless by the unanimous khaki color of the desert, building and mountain.[19]

Paglen often captures these images with what he calls "limit telephotography," using a telescopic lens powerful enough to photograph extraterrestrial images; however, even with a strong lens, he experiences difficulty capturing sites only twenty to fifty miles away. *Illuminated Hangars/Tonopah Test Range, NV/Distance ~18 miles/9:08 pm* of 2005, shows four outdoor lamps casting a sliver of light across a blackened, industrial lot. Contrary to the terrain's seemingly non-descript appearance, the title indicates that this image is from the Tonopah Test Range in south-central Nevada, a site once used for testing rockets and nuclear weapons in the 1950s, which is now an air force base committed to underground military operations. Paglen's use of informative and direct titles, a strategy of identification, counteracts the blurred hangar shapes and darkened areas that limit the observer's capacity to mine the details of the image. Rather than aim for visual specificity, Paglen's practice gestures at the difficulty of making visible something that is rendered invisible by deception.

Whereas the works of Lombardi and Paglen depict the fragmented body of privatization through flowcharts and counter-reconnaissance, the works of Ben Rubin and the Bureau of Inverse Technology address the often ignored subject of civil liberties in the face of privatization. Despite the mounting commercialization of the Internet, evidenced by proliferating information-based companies and their battles over web addresses and advertising space, the Internet's origins can be traced to the state's military defense strategy against nuclear attack in the late 1950s. Following the belief that, "if there are no central command centers, then there can be no central targets and overall damage is reduced,"[20] the Internet became the military's structural solution to protect the command and control centers against cold war enemies. While "the control of information has been, long before the information age, the foundation of state power,"[21] this control changed hands when the Internet gained a public face in the 1990s.

The promise of the Internet meant possible liberation of information from the confines of physical space and the fluid circulation of knowledge beyond national borders. This unprecedented level of connectivity also produced a tone of paranoia, evident in theorist Emily Apter's description of today's "'delirious aesthetic of systemacity,' a notion of *oneworldedness* that refutes the possibility of difference and insists that 'everything is connected."[22] Inciting both euphoria and apprehension, the initial discourse surrounding virtual space did not embrace how this territory—predicated upon accessibility—could produce advanced structures of ownership and surveillance. The Internet facilitates the free exchange of replicated content that challenges traditional ownership while permitting constant and inexpensive monitoring of users' behavior that pushes the boundaries of our "right to be let alone."[23] Neoliberals take great interest in this abysmal resource of information about the public's activities because of its potential to influence decisions in the global marketplace.

The Bureau of Inverse Technology (BIT), an artist collective composed of agents Natalie Jeremijenko and Kate Rich, investigates corporations that profile civilians by recording their behaviors in datasets that are easy to store, exchange, and merge. Acting as a "private information agency,"[24] BIT used a miniature spy plane to produce aerial views of restricted, no camera zones in the Silicon Valley. Scanning the corporate headquarters of Lockheed Martin, Yahoo, Xerox Parc, and more, the resulting thirteen-minute single channel video, *Bit Plane*, offers disorienting black-and-white footage that reveals a striking imbalance between the power and knowledge of companies known for monitoring public minutiae and the power and knowledge of the public whose counter-surveillance can come no closer than distinguishing one company rooftop from the next. In the work, Silicon Valley appears to be a mundane industrial complex partitioned by highways, parking lots, and recreation centers, but the editorial text dispersed throughout the footage informs of a "potentially hostile territory"[25] founded upon dot-com industries and data research centers. Whereas monitoring phones and postal mail would require human participation, massive storage facilities, and legal warrants, the structure of the Internet enables search-based "hollow corporations,"[26] like Yahoo, to complete virtual surveillance that would otherwise be unlawful in real life. In this "virtuous circle," where, "more searches produce more data, which attract more advertising dollars,"[27] the lure of profit upstages the safeguards protecting citizenship as more and more intricate

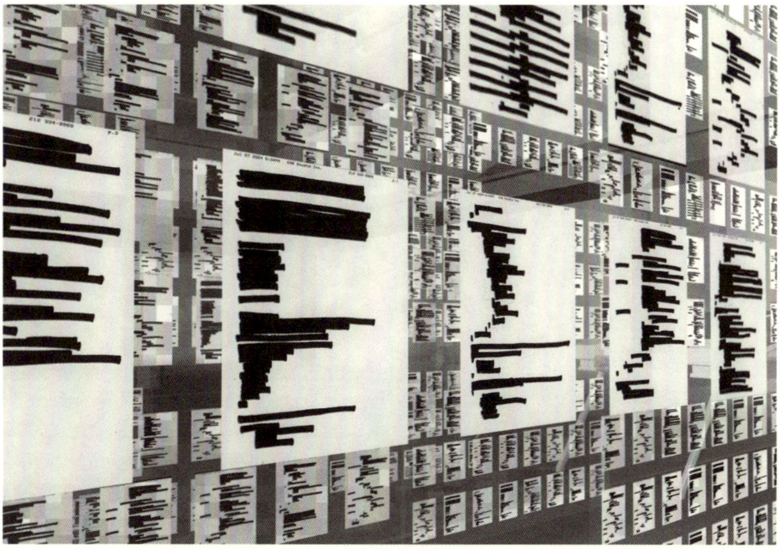

Ben Rubin, digital rendering for *Dark Source*, 2005

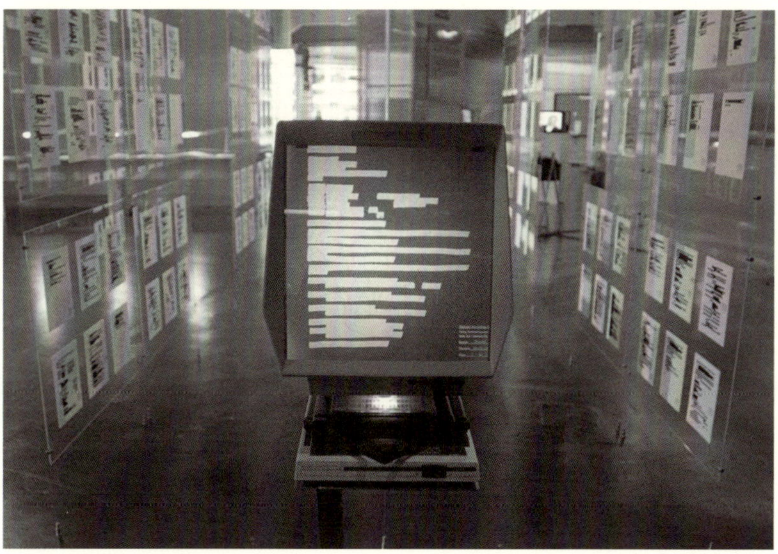

Ben Rubin, *Dark Source*, 2005

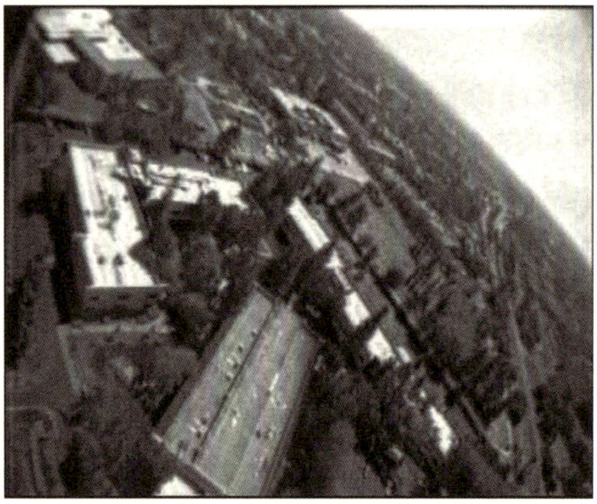

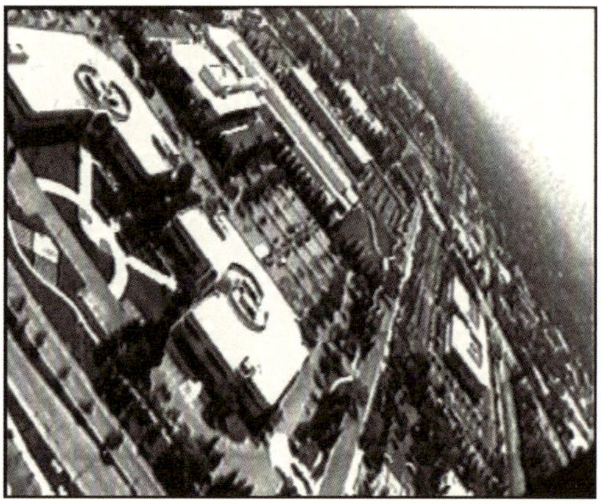

BIT recorded the activity over Lockheed Missiles & Space, Hewlett Packard, and the legendary Highway 101.

tools are developed to profile users' behavior as well as aggregate and share that data.[28]

Akin to pilot announcements, the narrative text of *Bit Plane* identifies one of the "sleek corporate campuses" with "artificial irrigated lawns"[29] to be Lockheed Martin, the "largest employer of Silicon Valley." Once responsible for creating the super-sector U-2 spy plane in the mid-1950s, Lockheed is now recognized for running a full gamut of electronic management for the government: "[Lockheed] sorts your mail and totals your taxes. It cuts Social Security checks and counts the United States census. It runs space flights and monitors air traffic. To make all that happen, Lockheed writes more computer code than Microsoft."[30] The irony of Lockheed's slogan "We Never Forget Who We're Working For" is how the intended answer of "the public" can now be seen in the shadow of *the government*. When government refutes its inherent role as proxy representative of the people, political activist Arundhati Roy claims that "to snatch [public assets] away and sell them as stock to private companies is a process of barbaric dispossession on a scale that has no parallel in history."[31] This dispossession is not only a disservice to the public, but it also plants the seeds for governmental destruction in which the government no longer has the means to solve problems without this fourth corporate branch.[32] While corporate agendas often exclude, or refuse to address, civilian liberties, they do take advantage of the public's waning confidence in today's government and carry out the tasks that government once set out to perform.

Rubin's *Dark Source*, a modified version of his large-scale installation of 2005, formally presents hundreds of pages of blacked-out software code from the AccuVote-TS voting machines produced by Diebold, a telecommunications company known for manufacturing safes and automated-tellers. Although Rubin located the entire code online during a 2002 security failure at Diebold, he marked out each line of the code to comply with corporate property rights and trade secrecy laws. Since the forbidden source code would remain incomprehensible to most even if exposed, Rubin's work is largely symbolic of "the state of affairs in which we find ourselves today, one in which the critical infrastructure of democracy in the United States is becoming privately owned, and being private, is also being

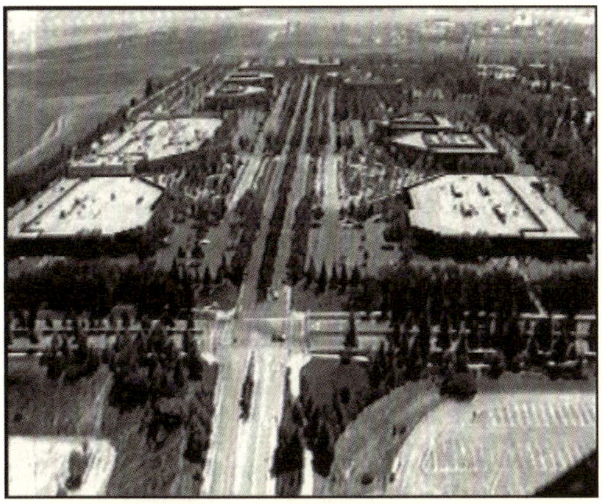

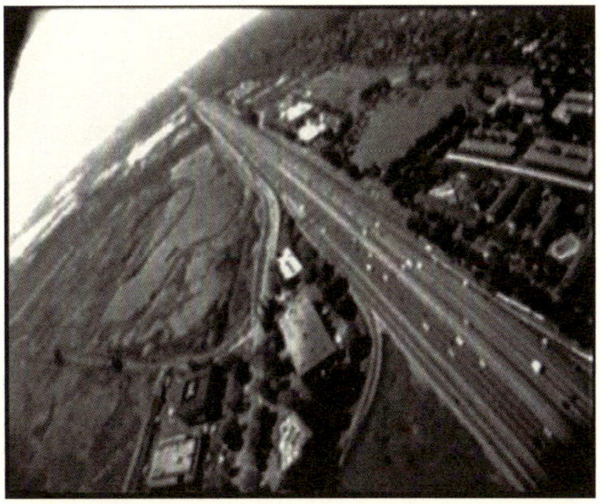

The Bureau of Inverse Technology,
Stills from *Bit Plane*, 1999

made secret."[33] His display of source code as a monolithic page-by-page grid hung from the ceiling, across three microfiche monitors, and projected as single documents is a metonym of the pervasive excess of control over information in modern society.

When the Help America Vote Act (HAVA), a legislative reaction to Florida's voting fiasco in 2000, allotted states 3.9 billion dollars in 2002 to upgrade their voting technologies, the four contending companies all proposed touch-screen machines to replace the punch-card and lever systems.[34] Despite the initial blind optimism for the success of these machines, the new technology did not materialize as expected: digital and paper records often do not match, printer jams occur frequently, and many poll workers and voters (especially senior citizens) are not equipped to manage the new technology.[35] Owning the code for voting technology (and its inevitable errors) proved to be a company's nightmare rather than a blessing.[36]

While law permits the state access to gambling software, the government cannot have access to this source code because of Diebold's right to safeguard its commercial position. Diebold's refusal to share its malfunctioning voting software with the public or the state that buys their machines endangers the process most basic to our democracy.[37] This hoarding of software secrets runs counter to the philosophy of software freedom activist Richard Stallman. His concept of the "data commons," an idea that emerged in the 1970s when "programmers would freely exchange and tailor pre-compiled source codes, improving and customizing them to suit their requirements."[38] By the 1990s, the enormous acceleration of the computer industry and its infiltration into everyday life made the opportunities for privatization visible. Companies responded by copyrighting their software and removing access to its source codes, essentially co-opting public ability to communicate within the "open source" domain. Copyright appears even more gratuitous in the case of the Internet and information technologies because "digital networks function by making 'copies'... every single use of creative work in a digital environment triggers, in theory at least, copyright."[39] When the state and its people are indiscriminately blocked from the open exchange of information, the groundwork is laid for an entire industry predicated upon secrecy and the violation of civilian privacy.

In February 2008, the *New York Times* reported that during Bush's eavesdropping program, telecommunications companies, who may (or may not) have provided information to the government, could be given retroactive immunity from prosecution. Even without immunity, the White House, invoking the privilege of "state secrets," would not confirm the identities of companies that cooperated with wiretapping, or release incriminating documents to the courts. The government's willingness to protect these companies, even if to defend and ensure the extension of its surveillance, establishes the principle that the power of corporations is more vital to this country than preserving the public's democratic "need to know."

While the works of Lombardi, Paglen, Rubin, and BIT deal with the restriction of information due to trade, state, or military secrets in today's privatized environment, the expansive difference in content between their works serves to illustrate the degree to which neoliberalism pervades our daily lives. The emphasis within these artistic gestures is not to actively "reclaim the commons" but to encourage the process of detecting signs of threatened civilian liverties. Through the visual constraints encoded in flow charts, blurry photographs, redacted code and surveillance footage, the artists reproduce the optical conditions of veiled information and invite us to consider the larger dilemma of how to increase the public's limited access to knowledge under conditions of corporate and government suppression.

NOTES

1. David Harvey, *A Brief History of Neoliberalism* (Oxford: Oxford University Press, 2005), 20.
2. Geographer David Harvey reasoned this majority to be "the white working classes and their besieged sense of moral righteousness (besieged because this class lived under conditions of chronic economic insecurity and felt excluded from many of the benefits that were distributed through affirmative action and other state programs)" in David Harvey, *Spaces of Global Capitalism* (London: Verso, 2006), 20.
3. Naomi Klein, *The Shock Doctrine: The Rise of Disaster Capitalism* (New York: Metropolitan Books, 2007), 6.
4. In *New York v. United States* (1985) the federal government tried to push responsibility of nuclear waste onto states proves that the federal government has a history of attempting to enact laws indirectly. According to Lawrence Lessig's interpretation of this case, "as independent sovereigns deserving of special constitutional respect," defended themselves against being "co-opted to the federal government's ends," insisting "that when the federal government has a program it wants to carry out, it must put its own name behind it" in Lawrence Lessig, *Code: Version 2.0* (New York: Basic Books, 2006), 133.
5. Hannah Arendt, *The Human Condition*, 2nd ed. (Chicago: University of Chicago Press, 1958), 200.
6. The Supreme Court's 1886 decision in *Santa Clara County v. Southern Pacific Railroad* claimed that as "persons, corporations should be protected by the Fourteenth Amendment's rights to 'due process of law' and 'equal protection of the laws,' rights originally entrenched in the Constitution to protect freed slaves" quoted from Joel Blakan, *The Corporation: The Pathological Pursuit of Profit and Power* (New York: Free Press, 2004), 16. Court cases from 1890 to 1910 show that lawyers at the time (ab)used this amendment, invoking it 288 times for business interests versus the nineteen times by African Americans.
7. When I use the term public, I refer to a group of people belonging to a political community whose membership affords a certain legal status (in this essay, I am only concerned with the American public).
8. Contrary to his signature style of large-scale flowcharts with perfect arcs and neatly organized compositions, *Neil Bush, Silverado, MDC* (discussed in the following paragraph) is much less manicured.

9. Robert Hobbs, *Mark Lombardi: Global Networks*, exh. cat. (New York: Independent Curators International, 2003), 27.

10. Pete Brewton, introduction to *The Mafia, CIA, and George Bush* (New York: S.P.I. Books, 1992), n.p.

11. Coinciding with this view of redistributed wealth were the words of journalist Orlando Letelier's 1973 report of Chile where neoliberal theory was tested for the first time: "concentration of wealth is no accident, but a rule; it is not the marginal outcome of a difficult situation—as the junta would like the world to believe—but the base for a social project; it is not an economic liability but a temporary political success" quoted from Klein, *The Shock Doctrine*, 86.

12. Hobbs, *Mark Lombardi*, 52.

13. Tan Lin, "Following the Money," *Art in America*, November 2003.

14. Mark Wigley, "Network Fever," *Grey Room 04*, Summer 2001, 111. This direct connection between his aesthetic and passion for information occurred as an organic result when in 1993 Lombardi attempted to visualize and make sense of his seven hundred-page manuscript *On Higher Grounds: Drugs, Politics, and the Reagan Agenda*.

15. Brewton, n.p. Brewton says that these CIA agents were known as "cutouts" and that the "the Mafia also makes use of such cutouts, except they call them as 'mustaches' or 'beards.'"

16. Giorgio Agamben, *State of Exception*, trans. Kevin Attell (Chicago: University of Chicago Press, 2005), 30.

17. Agamben, 24. It is interesting to note, as Arendt does, that "the Greeks derived their word for torture from *necessity*, calling it *anagkai*, and not from bia, used for violence as exerted by man over man" in Arendt, 129.

18. This rereading of the constitution, in terms unfavorable to the public, is an affront to Carl Schmitt's definition of the president as the "guardian of the constitution" as noted in Agamben, *State of Exception*, 15.

19. Because Paglen's work is considered to be counter-surveillance, there is no official proof of whether his photographs of black sites are manipulated or even true to their claims.

20. Alexander R. Galloway, *Protocol: How Control Exists After Decentrilization* (Cambridge: MIT Press, 2006), 29.

21. Manuel Castells, *The Power of Identity*, 2nd ed. (Oxford: Blackwell Publishing, 2004), 320.

22. Karen Beckman, "Telescopes, Transparency, and Torture: Trevor Paglen and the Politics of Exposure," *Art Journal 66*, no. 3 (Fall 2007), 66.

23. Todd S. Purdum, Jodi Wilgoren, and Pam Belluck, "Court Nominee's Life is Rooted in Faith and Respect for Law," *New York Times*, July 21, 2005. The court case *Olmstead v. United States* (1928) disputed a bootlegger's constitutional rights against a government that had wiretapped his telephone. As noted in the New York Times article, during the court case, Justice Braindeis is famous for saying that the framer's had "'conferred, as against the government, the right to be let alone—the most comprehensive of rights, and the right most valued by civilized men.'" This moment gave birth to the phrase "the right to be let alone."

24. Text from the website sponsored by the Bureau of Inverse Technology: http://www.bureauit.org/plane/

25. Text as appeared in The Bureau of Inverse Technology, *Bit Plane*, 1999.

26. Naomi Klein explains "hollow companies," to be similar to the "Microsoft model," whereby companies "maintain a tight control center of shareholder/employees who perform the company's 'core competency' and outsource everything else to temps, from running the mailroom to writing code . . . mostly form, with little tangible content left over" in Klein, *The Shock Doctrine*, 285.

27. Ken Auletta, "The Search Party," *The New Yorker* (January 14, 2008), 33.

28. For example, in January 2006, Yahoo and MSN a fulfilled Justice Department request that helped the Bush administration pass legislation against Internet pornography. While providing only one million random searches from its database, this gesture welcomes the government to demand more invasive searches in the future.

29. The Bureau of Inverse Technology, *Bit Plane*.

30. Klein, *The Shock Doctrine*, 293.

31. David Harvey, *The New Imperialism* (Oxford: Oxford University Press, 2003), 161.

32. For example, the ease of performing barely legal military procedures through corporations comes at the loss of the government's own intelligence. The director of national intelligence's account of the military modeling itself off of private companies, such as creating A-Space (an extension of My Space) and Intellipedia (derived from Wikipedia), is proof of its gradual decline against a better-equipped private sector. See Lawrence Wright, "The Spymaster: Can Mike McConnell Fix America's Intelligence Community?" *The New Yorker* (January 21, 2008), 50.

33. Ben Rubin, "Dark Source: Public Trust and the Secret at the Heart of the New Voting Machines," in *Making Things Public: Atmospheres of Democracy*, ed. Bruno Latour and Peter Weibel (Cambridge: MIT Press, 2005), 828.

34. Diebold's AccuVote-TS records votes according to what choices the voters tap on the screen, aggregating these votes on a flash-memory card as well as keeping a physical tally on a small printer next to the LCD screen. Prior to voting, the state decides which vote—the paper copy or the digital version—they will count.

35. Clive Thompson, "Can You Count On These Machines?" *New York Times Magazine*, January 6, 2008, 43-45. With a cover that reads, "Warning: Your vote may be lost, destroyed, miscounted, wrongly attributed, or hacked," the *New York Times Magazine* dedicated the cover story to voter machine technology, describing the many disappointments and failures since its inception in 2002.

36. As noted by Thompson, one analyst said that the voting machines were responsible for "five percent of revenue and one hundred percent of bad public relations." Thompson continues to discuss how Diebold did try "to sell off its voting-machine business, and, failing to find a buyer last August [2007] changed name of the division to Premier Election Solutions" in Thompson, "Can You Count," 43.

37. Diebold is a well-known and significant contributor to the Republican Party, a connection that inevitably casts suspicion on the many voter irregularities and tallies of George W. Bush's 2004 election victory.

38. Julian Stallabrass, "Digital Commons," *New Left Review* 15 (May-June 2002). For context, it should be noted that Richard Stallman is also responsible for the concept of "copyleft."

39. Lessig, *Code*, 268.

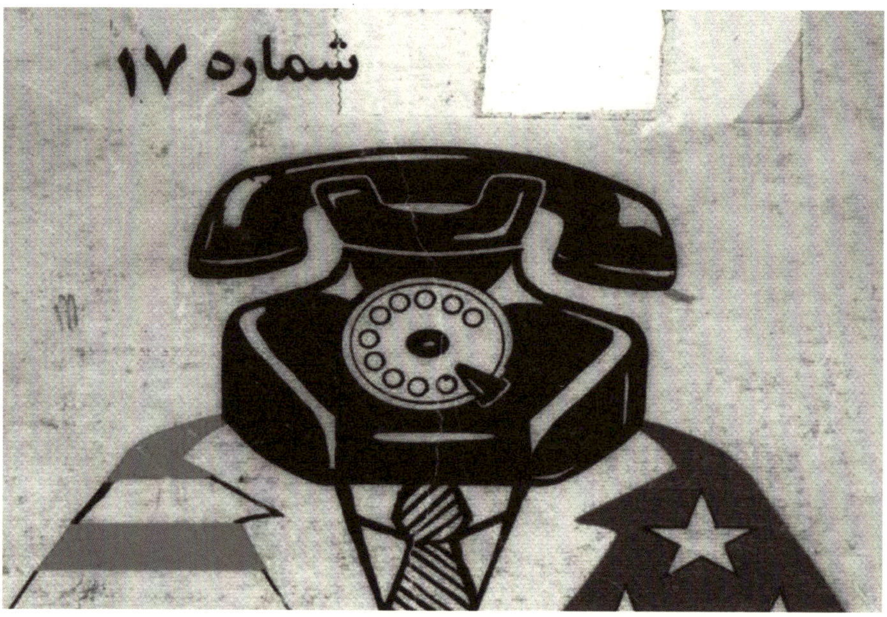

Speculative Archive (Julia Meltzer and David Thorne),
Still from *"It's not my memory of it": three recollected documents*, 2003

ESTIMATED ARCHIVAL TIME

Steven Lam

"IT'S NOT MY memory of it": three recollected documents, a video by Speculative Archive, contains interviews with intelligence officers discussing procedures of governmental declassification. In one sequence, Steven Garfinkel, Director of Information Oversight of the National Archives and Records Administration provides insight into the logic of modern intelligence systems. He states: "There are two types of secrets. There are real secrets, which are relatively few, things that one would assume are real secrets . . . then we also have a lot of secrets that I call protocol secrets." To clarify this enigmatic differentiation, he defines "real secrets" as new activities, new discoveries, or covert military operations such as weapons technology and research, and concealed diplomatic maneuvers. These secrets, limited in number, conceal specific intelligence, and their "secret-ness" often has a limited lifespan. On the other hand, "protocol secrets" are abundant and less overtly withheld from public transmission. "Everybody knows that it happens, we just can't admit that it happens." Garfinkel gives an illustration: "For example, we can't admit that we cooperate with another country in doing an intelligence operation against the third country. [Protocol secrets] are secret in the sense they are not admitted and so they are not formally true, it's just everybody assumes they're true."[1]

This notion of protocol secrets echoes the litany of "unknown unknowns," the numerous acts of doublespeak and disinformation removed from public purview that have occurred in the last thirty years: We "know" that the U.S. military frequently uses torture techniques, but the government has yet to admit it. We "know" that Iraq did not posses weapons of mass destruction, but the government has yet to admit it.

What Garfinkel's differentiation suggests is that secrecy has a form. It has a programmatic procedure and a temporal logic. The declassification of "real" secrets operates as a time- released mutation from dangerous (highly classified) to public clearance (ready for the history books). Secrets are classified, stockpiled, and organized within an archival structure. Here, "institutional and political memory, stored in vast white-collar fortresses," is accessed for its potential threat before being released to the public.[2] By contrast, protocol secrets hover in a state between confirmation and denial—conveniently malleable—awaiting refutation, verification, or eventual ejection from collective memory.

Historian, theorist, and scientist Peter Galison describes secrecy—a massive industry consisting of labor, research, and technology—as a by-product of World War II. The modern secrecy system blocks the transmission of knowledge through various classificatory and disinformation procedures. In his article, "Removing Knowledge," Galison details the bureaucratic administrative process that the Original Classifier within the Department of Defense undertakes in order to discern what information is classified and what information is ready to be disclosed. It is a simple process, almost algorithmic, that entails following a succinct list of instructions and questions such as: "Is the information owned by or under the control of the government?" and "Can the unauthorized disclosure of the information reasonably be expected to cause damage to national security?"[3]

Information, in the context of the contemporary "war machine" (the entire military intelligence apparatus), is not merely raw data, a field of facts, dates, and statistics that constitute knowledge. In the maneuverings of everyday war, information becomes an instrument of military knowledge: it is tactically assessed and distilled in the form of secret intelligence, serving the sole purpose of "knowing" the enemy.[4] These gatekeepers of information, Original Classifiers, are in the front line, developing strategies on how and when to release classified information, thereby occupying a position at a distant remove from the numerous agents that acquired the secret intelligence in the first place.

Acts of secrecy that block knowledge operate similarly to Jacques Derrida's definition of the archive with its attendant operations of recollection and repression. The archive is at once an architectural site, a repository of "facts" with defined physical limits as well as a procedure. To archive an object is to store and preserve it while simultaneously ascribing a system of order to it, placing it in a container and enclosing it. For Derrida, the "archons"—the rulers, or magistrates, who purport to create coherence out of the archive—are the first guardians of the documents. They not "only ensure the physical security of what is deposited and of the substrate," but they possess the "power to interpret the archives."[5] The Original Classifiers also possess the privileged position of archontic power; by classifying intelligence (thereby making it secret), information is made to conform to the laws of the archive.

Lin + Lam, Susan Schuppli, and Speculative Archive do not participate in a politics of exposure by reporting government secrets. Instead, they articulate another form of knowledge acquisition—one that prioritizes working backward, following paper trails, and perusing archives. However, the materials in question are specific archives from the recent past of the United States: abandoned espionage manuals, displaced propaganda films housed in the Library of Congress, and the Watergate files. Thumbing through an assortment of covert memorandums left from military officials, intelligence bureaucrats, or documents pilfered by "the enemy," the artists insist on constructing a larger picture from fragments and traces gathered through appropriation. They capture minute details that once held incriminating evidence, revealing the exclusionary principle of state archives and the slippage between knowledge and action. As Galison explains: "Epistemology asks how knowledge can be uncovered and secured, antiepistemology asks how knowledge can be covered and obscured. Classification, the antiepistemology *par excellence*, is the art of nontransmission."[6]

In the first section of Speculative Archive's *"It's not my memory of it": three recollected documents*: "Disclosure without Ceremony," an Iranian CIA informant, identified in the literature as SDURN, disappears in the documentation, which prompts an imaginary narration of SDURN's whereabouts and subsequent erasure. In 1986, a group of Muslim students in Tehran collected piles of shredded paperwork left after the abandonment of the U.S. Embassy in 1979. The students meticulously reassembled the documents, then published and distributed their contents in the seventy-seven-volume *Documents from the U.S. Espionage Den*. All traces of the CIA's activities are reported and presented as a whole. The documentation is extensive, ranging from banal telegrams that explain international tax regulations to speculations about the amount of oil in neighboring communist countries. The cryptic identity of SDURN and his role as a CIA source is also revealed.[7] In the video,

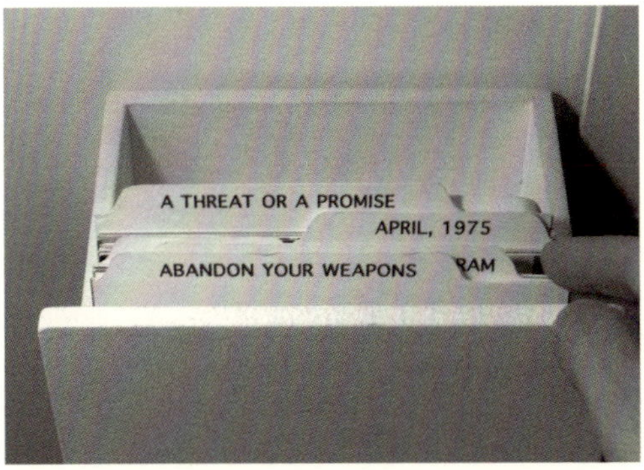

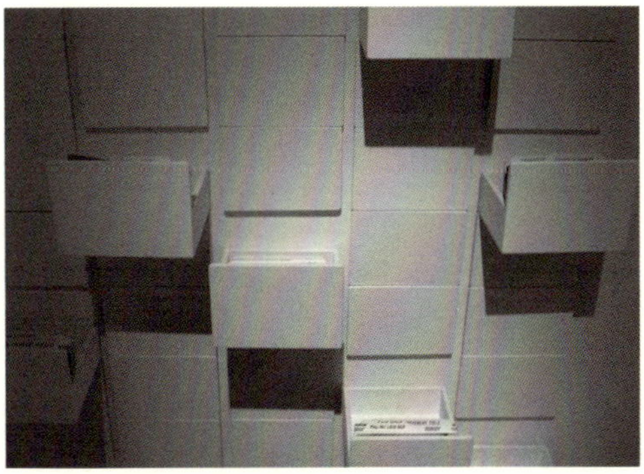

Lin + Lam, *Unidentified Vietnam No. 29*
(details of *Unidentified Vietnam* installation), 2006

pages from the appropriated book flicker before our eyes while strips from the cut-up documents are rearranged on the surface of the screen like a jigsaw puzzle. Errors in matching letters, punctuation, and sentences simulate the mutability behind this method of recovery, and the stuttering camera image attempts to articulate the unstable identity behind SDURN.

SDURN appears only a handful of times in *Documents from the U.S. Espionage Den*. For Speculative Archive, SDURN is an avatar, a vanishing cipher that haunts this cavernous "den" of codes and acronyms, clandestine reports and bureaucratic argot representing the discrepancy between official history and memory. As the video states: "In this collection of documents there is a memory of my disappearance that is not mine. I have a memory of it, but this one is an official record."

In 1968, a Soviet submarine sank in the Pacific Ocean and the United States launched a series of campaigns to stealthily salvage its remains. Hoping to recover cryptographic machines, nuclear warheads, and other intelligence on board the submarine, the government was only able to find missiles and six dead Soviet marines. As a result of their findings, the government conducted and filmed a ceremony for the deceased seamen on board the *Glomar Express*, titled *Burial at Sea*. But this documentation was never televised nor given to the Soviet state until 1992.[8]

Only the first portion of this "burial" footage was appropriated in *"It's not my memory of it."* Grainy and eerily shot, the footage seems more akin to an amateur home video than a soldier's funeral. A stationary camera focuses on an interior space (the hull of the ship). The shot, divided by the hanging flags of both nations, documents a clergyman who gives a eulogy. The shot eventually cuts to a sequence of a crane as it places the coffins in the sea. As opposed to the previous section in *"It's not my memory of it,"* this portion of the video slowly lets the footage run its own course; it is presented without any authorial intervention. Through this literal replaying of the "ceremony" the video articulates the awkward construct of this historical document. Like the rest of *"It's not my memory of it,"* this appropriation of the footage suggests an operation in which the reframing of the documentation is more than merely an act of renegotiating evidence. Here, documents have an afterlife; scraps of discarded manuals and video clips pulled from cold storage may not be intelligible in the present, but they carry a promise for the future.

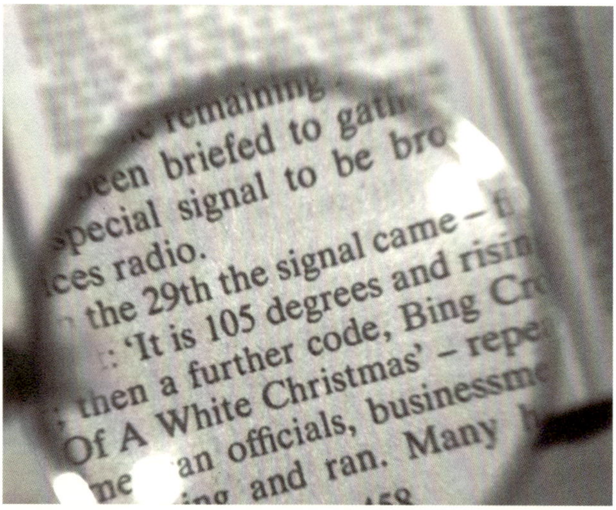

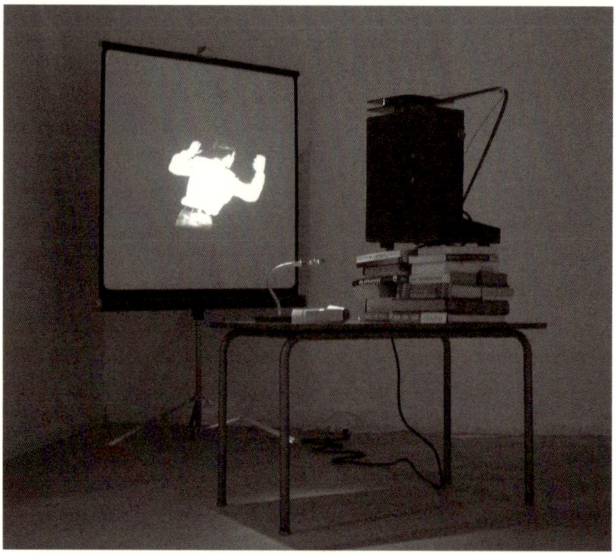

Lin + Lam, *Pupils of Democracy*
(details of *Unidentified Vietnam* installation), 2006

It would be inaccurate to equate files with memory. A file is merely a symbolic placeholder for the event. Burning, tearing, or shredding files in fear of their publicity does not guarantee the repression of memory: it does not return us to its original state of its history.[9] The destructive acts instigated against files merely substitute the erasure with an absence that could not be filled. Today, information is cross-indexed and perpetually linked. Voids, gaps, and erasure have more signification than the removal of its contents. Missing files may not be fully retrievable, but disappearances are easy to spot. Lin + Lam and Susan Schuppli tackle this notion of absence and the residual haunting that occurs with the memory of an erased file.

After the fall of Saigon in 1975, the United Stated recalled nearly 527 propaganda films that were made, distributed, sanctioned by the U.S. government prior to the Vietnam War. At that time the films, documents, and articles were stored within the South Vietnamese Embassy (SVNE). Following the dismantling of the embassy, the United States collected all the documents and shipped them to the Library of Congress for fear of having the documents fall into the hands of the communists. The films were a result of an elaborate cold war nation-building campaign in which agents distributed documents and films intended to modernize and educate the Vietnamese population. The documents are thus evidence of the propaganda that the United States employed to subvert and squelch the rising communist insurgency. This is echoed in *Pupils of Democracy*, a film installation that reassembles materials found in classrooms such as a kindergarten desk, a stack of books, and a film projector screen.

If state archives script and reinforce official histories, what type of narrative does the SVNE archive offer? Why would the United States not destroy the archive if it provides a testament to the U.S. role prior to the war in Vietnam as well as its subsequent failure?[10] What do we learn when the contents of an archive never intended to be seen by others than its target audience are revealed to the American public? This is precisely what is at stake with Lin + Lam's installation and film, *Unidentified Vietnam*, which appropriates contents from the SVNE. As the artists have frequently stated, the project begins with an ending. April 29, 1975, signaled "the end of the Vietnam War, the end of South Vietnam, the end of the U.S. military presence in Vietnam, the end of false hopes of democracy," as well as "the beginning of exile for millions of refugees, the beginning of the Socialist Republic of Vietnam."[11] After its initial transport, the SVNE archive fell into structural chaos. The films are mislabeled and inaccurately indexed in the Library of Congress. Paper tags are peeling off the canisters. This state of entropic disarray contributes to the suspension between evidence and event, fragmentation and reconciliation, history and memory.

Unidentified Vietnam No. 29 is an installation that mirrors a card catalog frequently found in the Library of Congress. Consisting of hundreds of photographs and excerpts from interviews, *UV no. 29* houses ethnographic research within an elaborate installation that enacts the operation of archival recovery. On the front of the index cards are photographs of doorways, hallways, architectural facades from the Library of Congress, as well and artifacts within the SVNE archive. The back of the cards cite excerpts from firsthand accounts and conversations with Library of Congress staff as they relate to this period of Vietnamese history. Individuals were asked to identify the various activities that were staged and documented in the propaganda films. The stammering moments of identification and recognition are captured in the interview and then transcribed on the card's reverse side: "This one is very familiar to me," one person recounts, or "That's the symbol on a jeep that I saw in Vietnam." However, *Unidentified Vietnam No. 29* is not meant to resolve a collective historical trauma by sealing the wound with authentic accounts of remembrance (despite the fact that these memories counter official history). Interspersed between the interviews are quotes taken from a variety of sources, including Henry Kissinger, Martin Luther King Jr., encyclopedic texts, and political scientists, which throw into question the integrity of the archive as well as its structural logic. This confusion of sources reveals that the archive is built upon contradictions; it is not meant to recover what is missing or fragmented but to allow for the cracks in the logic of the archive, the "unidentified," to resonate. As theorist Una Chung suggests: "The adjectival 'unidentified' is here not as a provocation to identify. It is counter to the archive's ordering of space and time . . . engaging in an experimentation with modes of *un*identifying."[12]

A silent tape lies buried in the vaults of the U.S. National Archives and Records Administration (NARA). It has been there for more than thirty years. Tape 342, just one tape out of the 3,700 hours of audio from the Nixon White House tapes contains the erased 18½ minutes that potentially incriminated the former president during Watergate. In April 1974, the House Judiciary Committee subpoenaed the entire collection of conversations President Nixon feverishly recorded and collected since 1972. This collection of tapes detailed various conversations with political opponents and guests at the White House. Tape 342, also known as the smoking gun, which was recorded just three days after the break-in at the Democratic National Headquarters. Responding to the subpoena, the White House provided lengthy transcripts of the collection but refused to provide the actual tapes. However, the court subpoenaed again and Nixon was forced to comply.

The first time Nixon's secretary, Rose Mary Woods, testified in court on November 8, 1973, she was questioned with the intention of determining whether she was responsible for the 18½ minute gap in Tape 342 after she transcribed the tapes. She asserted her secretarial competency: "The buttons said on and off, forward and backward. I caught on to that fairly fast. I don't think I'm so stupid as to erase what's on a tape."[13] However, later when she testified in front of a federal grand jury, Woods's story changed drastically. She admitted that she possibly made "a terrible mistake." While transcribing the tape with her UHER transcription machine (in an attempt to gather materials for the first subpoena), Woods claimed that the phone rang and that it was her attempt to reach across the desk, stretching to pick up the phone that caused the "accidental" erasure of the 18½ minutes. As farcical as her explanation may seem, this incident, burnt into government records, provides the only alibi for Nixon's supposed innocence.

Susan Schuppli's video and installation revisits this contentious moment. She displays a succession of photographs detailing the various artifacts that represent the scandal—two magazines with Woods on the cover, article clippings, a model of her transcription machine, the tape that "stores" the 18½ gap, and an enlarged photograph of Woods rehearsing her notorious stretch during the media blitz—are placed within an image timeline. Flanking the images is a quote by Nixon in 1957: "Next to a man's wife, his secretary is the most important person in his career. She has to understand every detail of his job; to have unquestioning loyalty and absolute discretion. On every count Rose measures up. I'm a lucky man."[14]

Adjacent to the photographic installation, a video features various secretaries reenacting and re-performing the "Rose Mary stretch." Executed in a deliberate flat, or uninflected, fashion, the video contains numerous sequences of

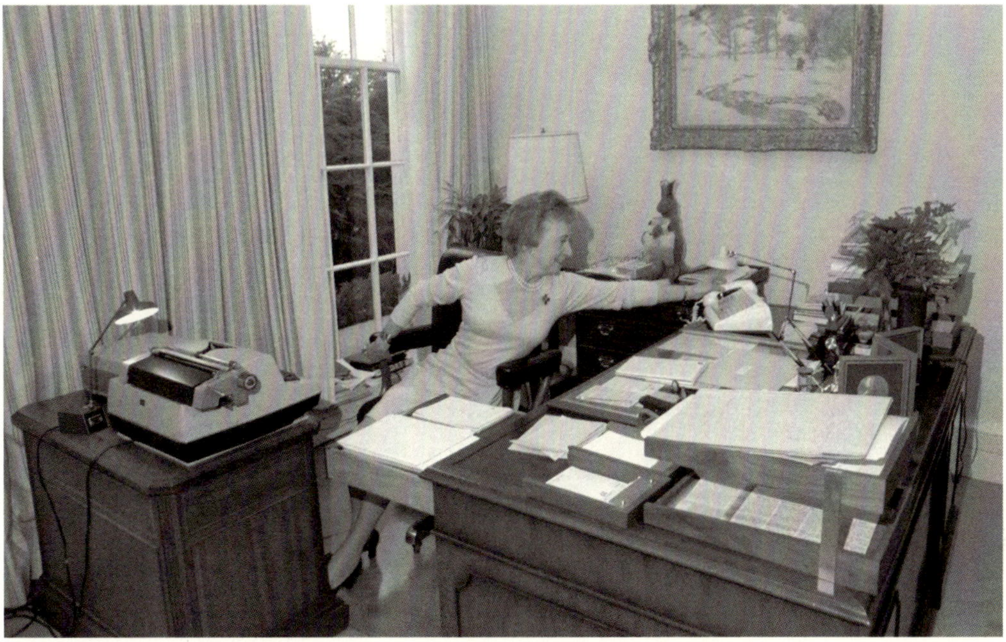

Susan Schuppli, *Stretch* (detail), 2007–08

contemporary women in similar workplace environments. A reenactment encodes the past into the present by making a perfect replica of the historical moment. Here this doubling is already implicated because the photograph itself is a reenactment, a staged recreation of this "accidental erasure." Within the context of Schuppli's larger installation, the dormant relics of the past reveal the thinly veiled relationship between the past and the present. The word secretary, as Schuppli indicates, "etymologically speaking means the 'keeper of the secrets.'"[15]

In 2001, NARA attempted to recover the 18½ gap in the tapes. Using highly specialized acoustic technologies, no methods have been able to resuscitate the contents of the tape. While this failure to retrieve the 18½ minutes upholds Nixon's innocence, it articulates the relationship between the artifact and archival time. Schuppli notes that media artifacts are *radioactive*: "Radioactivity asserts the artifact's capacity for continuous existence in the present and beyond. Its contaminating potential suggests that its toxicity will continue to effect and modulate the temporal zones through which it moves."[16]

All the artifacts displayed in Schuppli's timeline are stand-ins, props, and doubles that point to this moment of uncertain historical occurrence. Captured and gathered within this grid of photographs and video reenactments, each document is digitized, their analogical format replaced with the infinite reproducibility of the ones and zeros of digitized data streams. Even the 18½ minute gap is translated. Extracted from the NARA archive, the 18½ minute gap that is inaudible to the human ear is uploaded onto a small LCD screen in which one can see the flickering oscillations of the WAV file. As a visual format, the 18½ minute gap graphically renders the buzzing of the tape noise betraying the notion that silence is

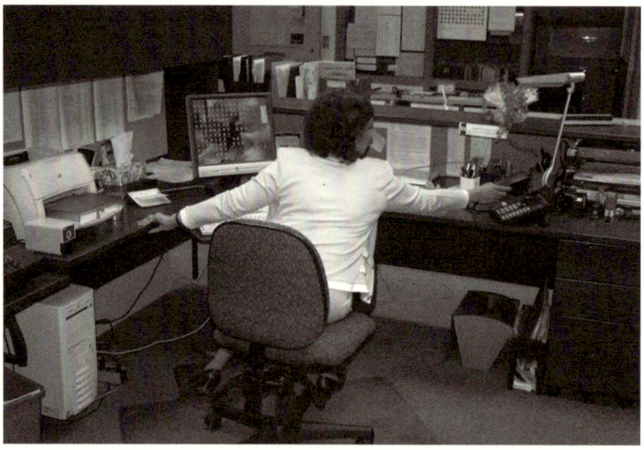

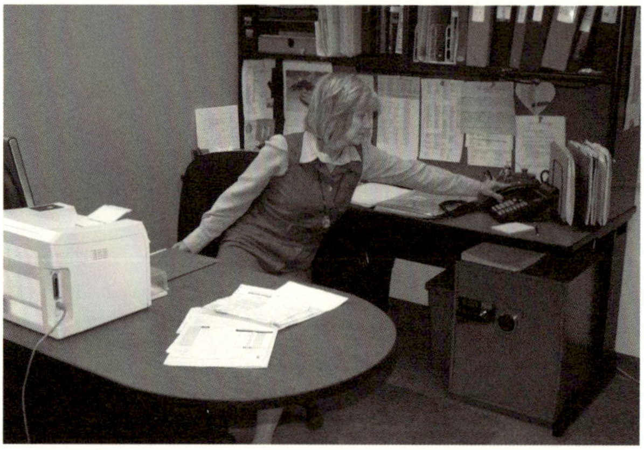

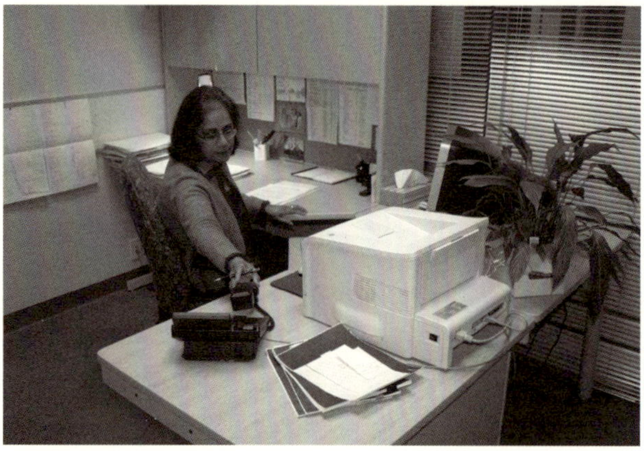

Susan Schuppli, Stills from *Stretch*, 2007–08

neutral. Imperfections are evident regardless of how careful the individual who seamlessly obscured the footage from the tape. The humming noise of the tape may not have been sufficient in providing the proper evidence against Nixon, but as phantom evidence, one that lies outside the juridical function, the tape awaits its moment when technological recovery is capable of removing the magnetic stain of its erasure.

In his article "Moblizing Shame," theorist Thomas Keenan suggests that the once effective attempt to employ reason to intervene with acts of atrocity will have to be updated: "The aesthetic finds itself in extreme proximity to the ethical-political now."[17] By appropriating and tracing documents, the works by Julia Meltzer and David Thorne, Lin + Lam, and Susan Schuppli suggest that despite the current regime of secrecy and opacity, artistic production provides a way to speculate and materialize the hidden and the unknown. If the secret impedes and blocks democratic deliberation, these practices mirror processes of declassification, offering methods in discussing a form of "politics beyond evidence."[18]

NOTES

1. From Speculative Archive (Julia Meltzer and David Thorne), *"It's not my memory of it": three recollected documents*, 2003.
2. John Menick, "The Art of Forgetting," *Parachute* 119 (Fall 2005), 105.
3. Peter Galison, "Removing Knowledge," *Critical Inquiry* (Fall 2004), 235.
4. Within the purview of military and political intelligence, "intelligence is the endeavor of knowing the enemy, identifying internal and external, visible and invisible, latent or manifest enemies, suspicious groups, and unstable alliances." In Eva Horn, "Knowing the Enemy: The Epistemology of Secret Intelligence," *Grey Room* 11 (Spring 2003), 61.
5. Jacques Derrida, *Archive Fever*, trans. Eric Prenowitz (Chicago: University of Chicago Press, 1995), 2.
6. Galison, "Removing Knowledge," 237.
7. The book is available in most university libraries and the contents can be downloaded from the Internet. The den refers to the nickname that the local population gave to the former embassy—the bunker of government secrets that detailed and profiled the local population.
8. The intention behind filming the ceremony is ambiguous and unclear. Perhaps the film served as an alibi confirming that the ceremony did in fact take place, that the government was not there to salvage the wreck but to set forth proper burials for the six men. In the 1990s, CIA director Robert Gates gave this undisclosed film to Boris Yeltsin further relinquishing any accusations of espionage while offering a symbolic gesture of reparation marking this event as the end of the cold war. As it turns out the footage of the "burial" does not reside in the public domain but is currently owned by ABC News; Meltzer and Thorne purchased six minutes of the footage at twenty-three dollars per second from ABC News as noted in John Menick, "The Art of Forgetting," *Parachute* 119 (Fall 2005), 106-8.
9. According to historians, the murderers who plotted to kill Julius Caesar were not satisfied with his death, but they wanted a complete ejection of the man from collective memory. The question posed to them was "how to extinguish Caesar's consulate ex tunic, how [can they] undo his political deeds from his rise to power to his death." After his assassination in an attempt to expunge any traces of Caesar, the plotters set his consulate files on fire. But this display of *damnatio memoriae*—the act of removal from remembrance—instigated and cultivated curiosity and inquiry rather than suppression and deletion thus reinforcing the role of the archive with the construction of historical memory. "The murderers of Julius Caesar tried to eliminate the files in the real in order to extinguish the unwanted data within the symbolic . . . they misunderstood the logic of disappearance" in Cornelia Vismann, "Out of File, Out of Mind" in *New Media Old Media: A History and Theory Reader*, ed. Wendy Hui Kyong Chun and Thomas W. Keenan (New York: Routledge, 2005), 98.
10. Perhaps I underestimate that modern states feverishly archive all their activities regardless of their clandestine nature and prioritize the preservation of these notes; the amount of labor that goes into disposing an archive as extensive as this one; the risk of losing a document if such measures are employed.
11. Ayreen Anastas, "Interview with Lin + Lam," *Artwurl* (Fall 2006), www.artwurl.org.
12. Chung, Una, "What. Comes. After.: An introduction to Lin + Lam's Unidentified Vietnam," *Art Journal* (Fall 2007), 22.
13. "The Secretary and the Tangled Tapes," *Time*, December 10, 1973, 15.
14. Ibid.
15. Susan Schuppli, "Curse of the Mummy," *Voodoo Space: Entangled Media Events* (unpublished PhD Thesis, Goldsmiths, University of London, 2008).
16. Susan Schuppli, e-mail message to the author, February 22, 2008.
17. Karen Beckman, "Telescopes, Transparency, and Torture: Trevor Paglen and the Politics of Exposure," *Art Journal* (Fall 2007), 64.
18. Ibid.

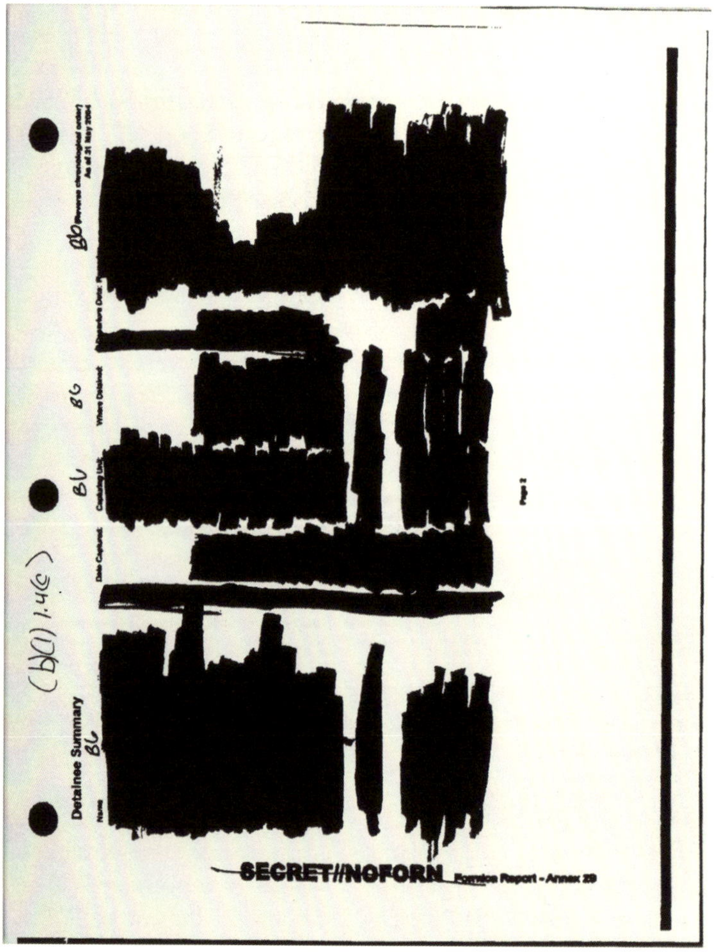

Jenny Holzer, *Small FORMICA 2851 YELLOW WHITE*, 2006

THE TRACE OF THE SECRET

Angelique Campens

A secret doesn't belong, it can never be said to be at home or in its place.
—Jacques Derrida

PUBLIC ACCESS to information is often determined by connections between political and corporate interests. These interests police what is seen and heard. Corporate ownership of information enables powerful institutions to limit access to data and other knowledge, while regulating what knowledge is disseminated through the media. In the United States, for example, major corporations have control over more than half of media businesses.[1] Ultimately, it is the media who decide when they keep a secret and what constitutes the history told in the future. A certain paradox is central to the media: they promote freedom of speech and suppress information.

As Stuart Hall states: "It [media] is ideological because it offers a partial explanation as if it were a comprehensive and adequate one—it takes the part for the whole (fetishism). Nevertheless, its legitimacy depends on that part of the truth, which it mistakes for the whole, being real in fact, and not merely a polite fiction." He argues further that the media "freely articulated themselves systematically around the definitions of the situation which favored the hegemony of the powerful."[2] This is compounded by the conditions we live in, where government secrecy is taken for granted. And when things are secret, society cannot take care of them or be responsible for them. But in a democracy every citizen needs to be responsible.

Jacques Derrida argued: "There is no political power without control of the archive, if not of memory. Effective democratization can always be measured by the essential criterion: the participation in and the access to the archive, its constitution, and its interpretation."[3] Or, as Hannah Arendt puts it, "Real power begins where secrecy begins."[4] But how can we keep a secret in an open society? There is a growing assumption that with the rise of the Internet, our society becomes more transparent; Google and YouTube spell the end of secrecy. This idea was evidenced in images of the execution of Saddam Hussein, which were widely disseminated through the Internet.

Digital technology has the power to make us believe in the end of secrecy. As Jodi Dean writes, "Now everybody knows, and the technologies believe for us: we don't have to believe each other; we can search and link and find the truth that is out there."[5] On the other hand, such a belief in the transparency of technology perhaps plays into the hands of the powers-that-be. After all, the excess of information can often obscure the nature of the problem. We see Hussein killed, but there is little information about the formation of the lies that led the United States to invade Iraq in the first place. We think we know, but perhaps we only know what the institutions want us to know.

Artists such as Jenny Holzer, Ben Rubin, and Bik Van der Pol take aim at the heart of this

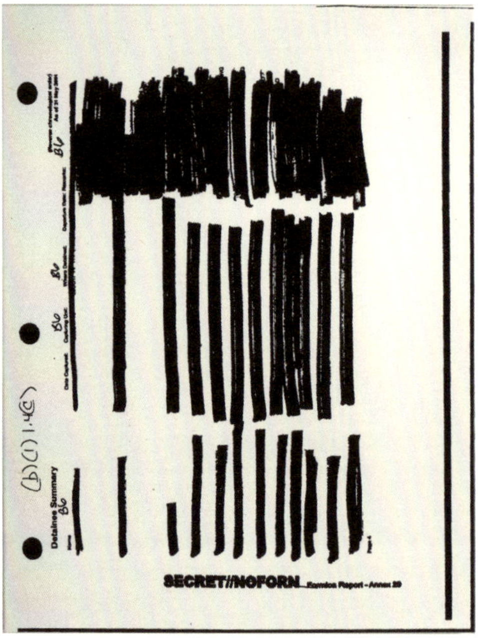

Jenny Holzer, *Small FORMICA 2853 YELLOW WHITE*, 2006

secrecy. They demonstrate that there are different methods of hiding a secret: disappearance, erasure, and burial. They also know that these erasures and disappearances occur in different media, ranging from the document to the photograph. In the realm of documents, the practice of "erasure" as a way of both making secret and interrogating the secret has a particularly important place in both art and critical theory.

Sous rature (under erasure) is a concept often used by Derrida. Gayatri Spivak explains the practice of *sous rature* in the following way: "This is to write a word, cross it out, and then print both word and deletion. (Since the word is inaccurate, it is crossed out. Since it is necessary, it remains legible.)"[6] Erasure is not entirely a process of elimination but of working through and interrogating the conditions and meanings created by the original document. Erasure is seldom only an act of letting things disappear since there is always a trace of the original. There is, furthermore, something desirable about the idea of an erased secret hiding between the lines.

The concept of sous rature also has an important history within the field of art. For example Honoré de Balzac's *The Unknown Masterpiece* (1837)[7] is about a painter, Frenhofer, who works for more than ten years on his masterpiece *la belle noiseuse*—a portrait of a woman. He spends so much time on it that the layers of paint pile up and the figure is no longer visible. As a result, the artist unintentionally produces the first abstract work. At the same time, the faint outline of the woman keeps her present, but only, as it were, *sous rature*.

Erasure can be seen as an addition, or as Jasper Johns put it, "additive subtraction" when referring to Rauschenberg's *Erased de Kooning Drawing* (1953).[8] In that work, Rauschenberg probed the possibility that "a drawing could be

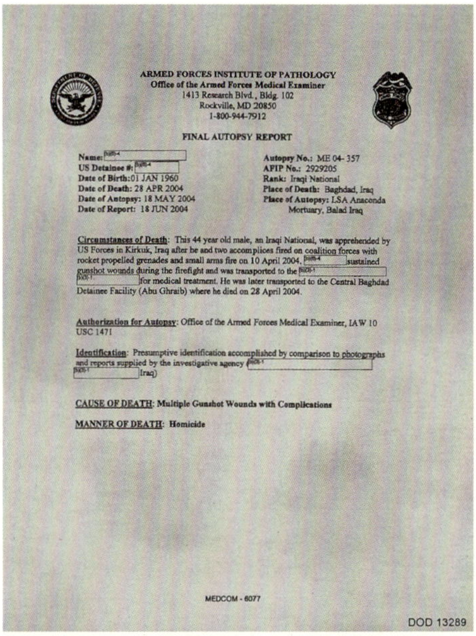

ARMED FORCES INSTITUTE OF PATHOLOGY
Office of the Armed Forces Medical Examiner
1413 Research Blvd., Bldg. 102
Rockville, MD 20850
1-800-944-7912

FINAL AUTOPSY REPORT

Name:
US Detainee #:
Date of Birth: 01 JAN 1960
Date of Death: 28 APR 2004
Date of Autopsy: 18 MAY 2004
Date of Report: 18 JUN 2004

Autopsy No.: ME 04- 357
AFIP No.: 2929205
Rank: Iraqi National
Place of Death: Baghdad, Iraq
Place of Autopsy: LSA Anaconda Mortuary, Balad Iraq

Circumstances of Death: This 44 year old male, an Iraqi National, was apprehended by US Forces in Kirkuk, Iraq after he and two accomplices fired on coalition forces with rocket propelled grenades and small arms fire on 10 April 2004. sustained gunshot wounds during the firefight and was transported to the for medical treatment. He was later transported to the Central Baghdad Detainee Facility (Abu Ghraib) where he died on 28 April 2004.

Authorization for Autopsy: Office of the Armed Forces Medical Examiner, IAW 10 USC 1471

Identification: Presumptive identification accomplished by comparison to photographs and reports supplied by the investigative agency (Iraq)

CAUSE OF DEATH: Multiple Gunshot Wounds with Complications

MANNER OF DEATH: Homicide

MEDCOM - 6077

DOD 13289

Jenny Holzer, *Final Autopsy Report DOD 13289 - DOD 13296 OCHRE*, 2006 (detail)

made out of erasing."[9] In this sense, Rauschenberg uses the eraser as a drawing tool, and by erasing the old drawing he is creating a new one. Erasure can thus be seen to add another layer on a work of art. Roland Barthes notes a similar phenomenon in the work of Cy Twombly where he, "seems to cover other strokes, as if he wanted to erase the latter without really wanting it, since these strokes remain faintly visible under the layer which covers them."[10]

The influence of Rauschenberg's *Erased de Kooning Drawing* can also been seen in many later artists, from Richard Hamilton's cover of the Beatles' *White Album* to Marcel Broodthaers's *La Pluie (Projet pour un texte)* (1969), where he filmed himself writing a text that is erased by the rain falling down on his paper, to Felix Gonzales-Torres's *Untitled (passport)* (1991), which is a stack of blank white paper. Erasure often connotes repression, either psychological or political. But these examples show that erasure (emphasizing the trace) is different from erasing (repressing the trace). As with Derrida, these art pieces show that erasure is about critical tactics and alternative ways of producing meaning. These "formalist" erasures thus help elucidate the importance of the procedure.

One way to understand some of the works in this show is to investigate the relationship between art and documents. "The Thirteen Theses against Snobs" in Walter Benjamin's *One Way Street* (1928) confronts the artwork with the document by dividing the page into two columns with left side bearing the qualities of an artwork and right side the qualities of a document. He then meditates on this juxtaposition. He claims in the second thesis that "the artwork is only incidentally a document" and "no document is, as such, a work of art." In his twelfth thesis, Benjamin claims, "the masculinity of works lies in assault" while "the document's innocence gives it cover." By assault he could mean that art grabs our attention through what Benjamin elsewhere calls the "shock"–the moment that opens the viewer to seeing something new; something which nevertheless remains undefined. Perhaps then what he means by the document's innocence is that it does not shock you but rather subtly wins you over and thus has greater ability to influence than a traditional work of art. Explicating Benjamin by way of a Kantian paraphrase, it could be said that art without documents is empty and documents without art are blind. Perhaps a synthetic moment is called for.

But what if art uses documents? What if documents are art? Can documents and art be attacking and, at the same time, convincing? Benjamin, in his second thesis, claims this is not possible, but there are artists who disagree. And the work of Jenny Holzer and Ben Rubin is a perfect example.

In her Redaction Paintings series, Jenny Holzer enlarges declassified documents from the U.S. National Security Archive and silkscreens them on linen. In these works, Holzer sheds light on heavily obscured information about military activity in Iraq. She fosters a debate about secret operations, ghost detainees, prisoner abuse, and war tragedies in Iraq, Afghanistan, and Guantanamo Bay out of the obscured past and into a critical present. The documents she uses consist of letters, emails, interrogation reports, as well as testimonies from prisoners, soldiers, and policy makers. The documents show the brutal narrative of physical and psychological maltreatment being deployed in the "war on terror." The most negative information crossed with black ink by the government shows us the mark of censorship.

One of the works from the Redaction Paintings series, *Formica Report*, consists of sixteen works in oil on linen. The Formica Report is a heavily redacted copy of seventy-five pages of classified documents where army Brigadier General Richard Formica had written his findings about detainee abuse by units in Iraq. (The Formica Annex [an addendum to the report] was composed in 2004 and released with many redactions by the Pentagon in 2006.) Holzer displays enlarged reproductions of some of the more than six hundred pages of the annex. Thanks to the Freedom of Information Act, the Pentagon's report is available to the public–as are thousands of other pages of government reports on the "war on terror"–but in a painful irony whole parts of the text were censored by the U.S. government prior to their release. In the Formica Report whole sections were redacted or blacked out, resulting in nothing but solid black blocks. Still visible are accounts such as that of a prisoner only being fed bread and water for seventeen days. Other detainees were locked in cells so small that they could neither stand nor lie down for as many as seven days. We can only imagine what lies behind the rest of the black rectangles.

At first sight, Holzer's *Formica Report* looks very formal and abstract, but when viewed more closely, a totally different layer of information is perceptible. Holzer's paintings take the documents that are often unseen and give visibility to a hidden past (in the present), and through their emphasis on redaction, she brings the process of censorship to light. Holzer's works are dialectical in the way that shows the declassified documents–including those that reveal the most painful abuse of power in Iraq–in a very seductive and desirable painterly surface. Through references to abstract painting, Holzer relies on this history of erasure in art going back to Rauschenberg, while forcing the practice to confront the documents of the present.

Ben Rubin's large-scale installation *Dark Source* consists of two thousand pages of blacked-out software code that Diebold–a telecommunications company recently hired

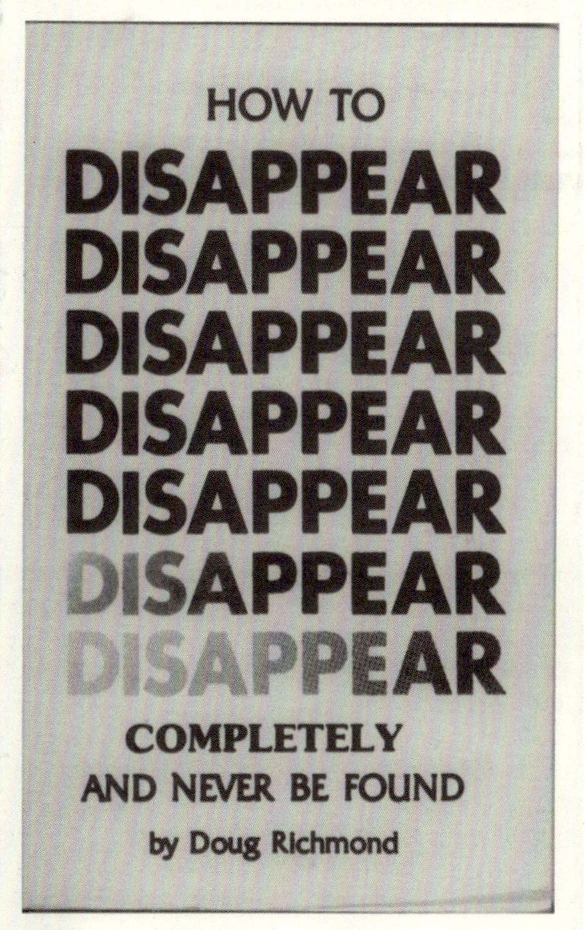

Bik Van der Pol, *The Disappearance Piece*, 2007
(detail of a facsimile of Doug Richmond's *How to Disappear Completely and Never be Found* [Port Townsend, WA: Loompanics Unlimited, 1986])

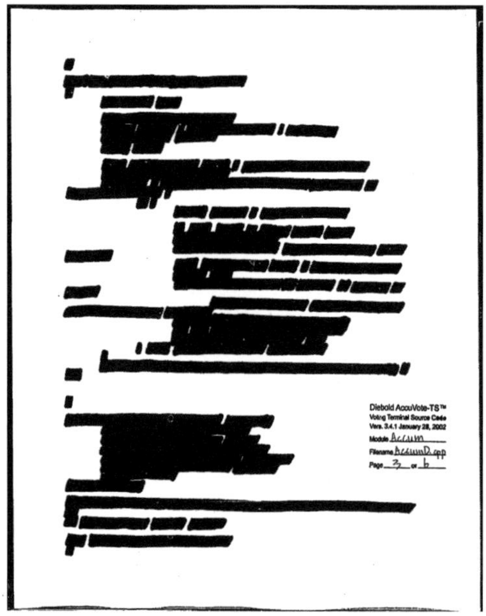

Ben Rubin, *Dark Source*, 2005 (projection detail)

by the federal government to manufacture touch-screen voting systems—concealed due to corporate property rights and trade secrecy laws. The installation shows a printout of Version 4.3.1 of the AccuVote-TS™ source code—49,609 lines of C++. Seven hundred and twenty pages of the printout are hung from the ceiling in plexiglass frames, and several hundred additional pages can be accessed on microfiche. Rubin obtained the code on the Internet because of a 2002 security failure, but due to the constraints of intellectual property rights, he was legally required to strike out each line. With *Dark Source* Ben Rubin questions how the ownership of information affects the public, and asks why corporations operating within the critical infrastructure of democracy manage knowledge that the state should control.

While Rubin and Holzer examine evidence that is proprietary or withheld (but whose veiled surfaces serve as sites for critical engagement), a more physical form of erasure can be found in Bik Van der Pol's *The Disappearance Piece*. This work consists of stacks of a fascimile of Doug Richmond's 1995 book *How to Disappear, Completely, and Never be Found*. The publication guides the reader through the mechanics of how to disappear without leaving tracks, and the author explains how you can efface your old life by faking suicide and then take a new identity. He continues with instructions about how to function in society without any background.

Bik Van der Pol presents the stacks of the books in the installation. Visitors take copies so that, as the exhibition progresses, the stacks begin to disappear, and the participants become collaborators in the work's disappearance. But it is not clear that visitors are allowed to take a copy since they are not explicitly told to do so. Taking a copy almost feels like stealing something. In this way, *The Disappearance Piece* is different than other take-away art practices (such

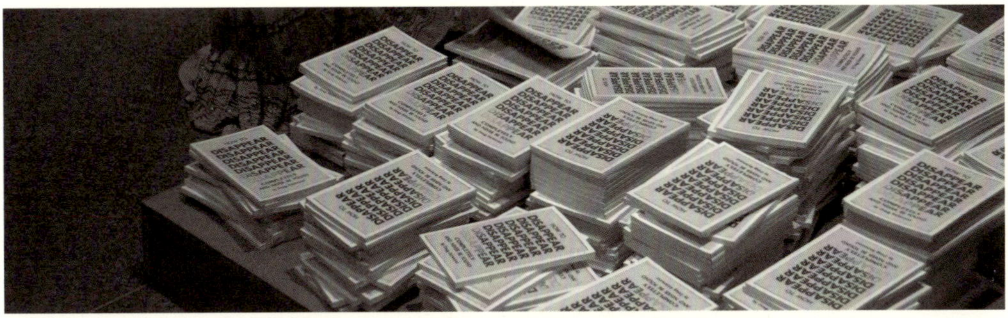

Bik Van der Pol, *The Disappearance Piece*, 2007 (installation view)

as the work of Felix Gonzalez-Torres or Rirkrit Tiravanija) where the concept of removal is central and the audience is invited to participate. Bik Van der Pol asks us to question our unacknowledged role in a world of disappearance. Do we, in our confusion about whether or not to participate in the disappearance, fail to act? Or, do we, in our insistence on appearing, proclaim a right of the state to police our identities? In other words, what is the difference between a right to disappear, a right to appear, and a right not to hidden by another? In any event, a physical disappearance may be a disappearance from the existing order, but disappearing is not literally vanishing from the world. As with the erasure of documents or words, some traces are always left behind.

Holzer, Rubin, and Bik Van der Pol show that a lot of vital information is not just hidden from our eyes, but it has been actively made to disappear. The practice of erasure—both in art and society at large—can help us to understand this process of secrecy and the importance of interrogating the secret. Appropriation thus becomes a means for artists to explore where secrets are being kept and allows them to intervene in this culture of secrecy. They remind us that although U.S. citizens live in a so-called transparent society with things like the Freedom of Information Act, many important documents are still hidden or heavily redacted before we see them. This secrecy questions the very foundation of the concept of freedom of information and even threatens democracy. Documents used to create art try to grab our attention, attack, and, at the same time, make us think about the relationship between secrecy and democracy.

NOTES

Epigraph. Jacques Derrida, *The Gift Of Death*, trans. David Wills (Chicago: University of Chicago Press, 1995), 92.

1. *Manufacturing Consent: Noam Chomsky and the Media*, directed by Mark Achbar and Peter Wintonick (Montreal: Necessary Illusions Productions, 1992).
2. Stuart Hall "The Rediscovery of 'Ideology': Return of the Repressed in Media Studies," in *Culture, Society and the Media*, ed. M. Gurevitch et al. (London: Methuen, 1983), 86.
3. Jacques Derrida, *Archive Fever, a Freudian Impression*, trans. Eric Prenowitz (Chicago: University of Chicago Press, 1996), 4.
4. Hannah Arendt, *The Burden of Our Time* (London: Secker and Warburg, 1951), 386.
5. Jodi Dean, *Publicity's Secret, How Technoculture Capitalizes on Democracy* (New York: Cornell University Press, 2002), 118.
6. Jacques Derrida, *Of Grammatology*, trans. Gayatri Chakravorty Spivak (Baltimore: Johns Hopkins University Press, 1976), xiv.
7. Honore de Balzac, *The Unknown Masterpiece*, trans. Richard Howard (New York: New York Review Books, 2001).
8. Jasper Johns, *Paintings, Drawings, and Sculpture 1954-1964* (London: Whitechapel Gallery, 1964), 27.
9. National Collection of Fine Arts, Robert Rauschenberg. (Washington, D.C.: Smithsonian Institution, 1976), 75.
10. Roland Barthes in *Cy Twombly: Painting and Drawings 1954-1977* (New York: Whitney Museum of American Art, 1979), 22.

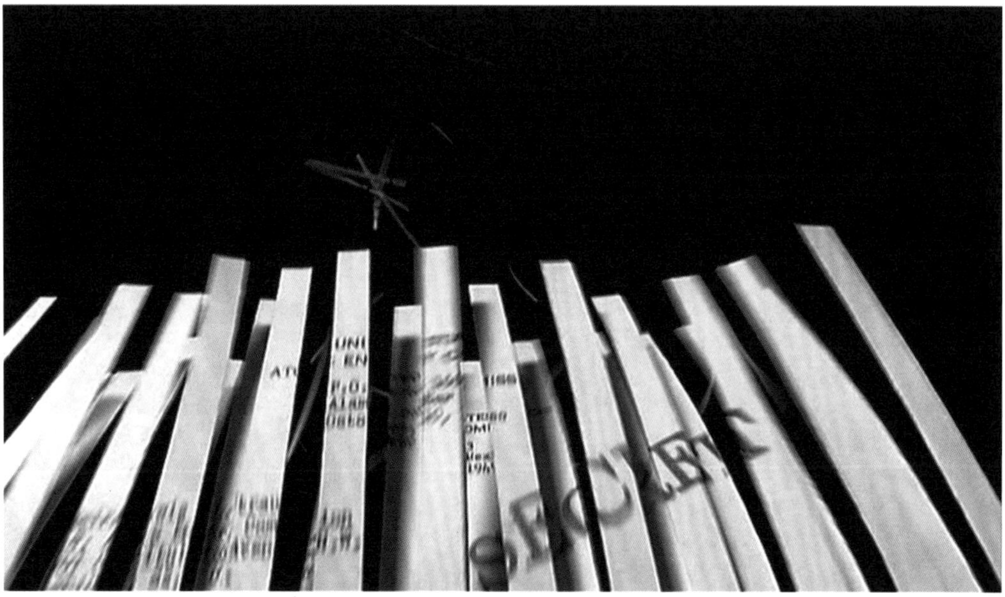

In a single recent year, the U.S. classified about five times the number of pages added to the Library of Congress. We live in a world where the production of secret knowledge dwarfs the production of open knowledge. —Peter Galison and Robb Moss, directors' statement from *Secrecy* (2008).

SECRECY

Conversation with Peter Galison and Robb Moss

PETER GALISON is Pellegrino University Professor of the History of Science and of Physics at Harvard University. His books include *How Experiments End* (1987), *Einstein's Clocks, Poincaré's Maps* (2003), and, most recently, *Objectivity* with L. Daston (2007); he has worked extensively with declassified material in his studies of physics in the cold war, including his film *Ultimate Weapon: The H-bomb Dilemma with Pamela Hogan* (2000). He has also contributed to the exhibition catalogue *Making Things Public: Atmospheres of Democracy* (2005) and co-curated *Iconoclash: Beyond the Image Wars in Science, Religion an Art* (2002) at ZKM, Karlsruhe, Germany.

ROBB MOSS is a documentary filmmaker and Rudolf Arnheim Lecturer on Filmmaking and Director of Undergraduate Studies in the Visual and Environmental Studies at Harvard University. Moss's film, *The Same River Twice*, premiered at the 2003 Sundance Film Festival, was nominated for a 2004 Independent Spirit Award, and screened in more than eighty cities across North America. Other films by Moss have been shown at the Telluride Film Festival in Colorado and at Lincoln Center and the Museum of Modern Art in New York, as well as numerous international venues.

Your film, Secrecy, *set for release prior to the 2008 presidential election, speaks to your respective practices in science and film. Can you please describe the documentary?*

PETER GALISON: Making *Secrecy*, Robb and I wanted something rather different; narrative, we thought, would throw the viewer of the film out of the world that we were trying so hard to enter. For the same reason—to draw people into this huge but hermetic universe of secrets—we wanted no pundits, no historians, no politicians. Instead, we were after the sealed-off feel of people working with, against, and skew to each other: agents and reporters, intelligence analysts, and ordinary folks swept up in the vortex of secrecy. That said, as in *Ultimate Weapon*, the film *Secrecy* moves from head-on confrontation to a reframing of the problematic of secrecy. First, it pulls us from the classical opposition, "more secrecy versus less secrecy" to questions of compartmented versus distributed information. Then, in the final third of the film, *Secrecy* aims to pull us into the halting, hard-fought task of mounting oversight as resistance to ever-more concentrated power.

ROBB MOSS: In style and approach, *Secrecy* is quite different than my previous work, which has been mainly in the form of autobiographical essays. As a filmmaker, how do you make sense of things you don't understand? This belief in the centrality of experience is also mirrored in the choices we made in whom to film. By choosing to interview practitioners rather than pundits, we hoped to populate our film with people for whom secrecy was a lived experience rather than simply a policy item, whose thoughts were their own rather than sound bites for our opinions. We chose to include relatively few interview subjects, and we let them take the time they needed to make their case. We wanted them to tell stories. In this way, we hoped to make the issues of secrecy not only consequential but personal as well. We are planning on making a short from either parts of our existing film or from new material that we could not fit into a beginning-middle-end structure, which we would distribute virally. The politics of a film reside not only in content and aesthetics but in its distribution strategies. We hoped to make a film that could be maximally repackaged and repurposed to reach as many people as we can.

As a professor in the history of science, can you elaborate upon the importance of visual documentation within scientific research?

PG: In my written work, images serve to get at the way scientists work, argue, and persuade. Images restore that placement of scientific practice and process—it should be central to our understanding of the history of science whether scientific workspaces more resemble churches, private homes, cottage industries, or massive factories. Sites matter because the practical conduct of science shapes how scientists see themselves and what they do—it shapes the roles they play politically and socially. Working under a high industrial bay with traveling cranes and the watchful eye of clipboard-toting safety officers is a very different mode of scientific life from the solitary enterprise of a lone researcher staffing a cosmic-ray outpost high up in the snow-blown mountains of Austria. Images can also convey evidence itself—in one of my books, *Image and Logic*, I was precisely tracking two enduring and powerful currents within modern physics—one that seeks evidence in counting, statistics, and logic, the other in those delicate tracks recorded on film from cloud chambers, bubble chambers and nuclear emulsions. In short, images in my writing aim to get at the constantly shifting ways of being-in-science—the historically located scientific self.

Your involvement as a writer and curator in exhibitions like Iconoclash *and* Making Things Public *is very unique. What are the political and social stakes with this type of interdisciplinary investigation?*

PG: As you mentioned, in my curatorial and film work, the aesthetic aspect of science and technology is not (for me) a question of admiring this or that scientific result. Scientific aesthetics are much more deeply embedded in process, in the nature of the work. Scientists have long understood this—every mathematics department in Europe and the United States used to have elaborate plaster, wire, and wood models of mathematical functions. Back in the latter part of the nineteenth century many mathematicians believed deeply that familiarity with these models would deepen understanding and eventually lead to discoveries. That enthusiasm dampened, but the impulse is interesting: aesthetics meant something more than abstract beauty—aesthetic judgment—for many scientists reached back to the older more tactile significance of the term. I like this material aspect of curating—it gives a chance to convey in more directly physical ways how scientific images and objects are mustered together into the work of discovery, demonstration, and persuasion.

Film for me extends these ideas. Physics in its current form cannot be understood as abstracted from power—A-bomb scientists like J. Robert Oppenheimer said, "physics have known sin"; more to the point, physicists have known power. And power is always, not just recently, bound up with control over image, force, scale, and . . . aesthetics. Grappling with the meaning of science today

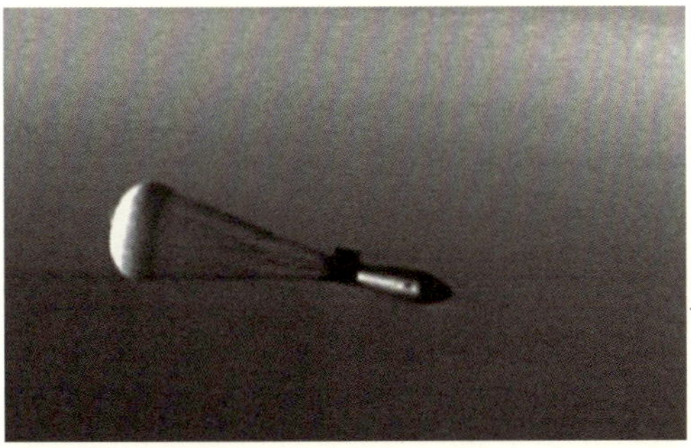

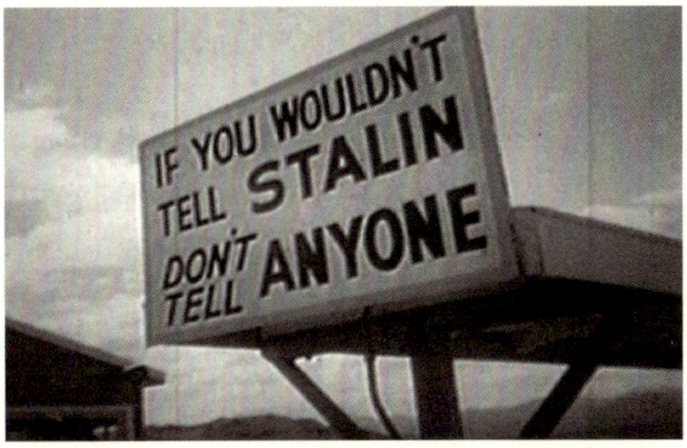

Stills from *Secrecy*, 2008

means grappling with its physicality, not least the simultaneous horror and seduction of nuclear weapons and facilities that are among the largest industrial sites ever created.

In Secrecy, *you mapped out the archaeology of secrecy through the overlapping sectors of science and military research. In the current administration, what parts of our society do you see as most reflective (or instrumentalized) by government policy?*

PG: There is knowledge which I think is rightly secret; I certainly don't want to see detailed instructions about how to make weapons of mass destruction distributed on the Internet as if they were e-postcards. Some of that secrecy has not fundamentally changed in many years—the Manhattan Project guarded A-bomb details during World War II, authority for it passed to the Atomic Energy Commission and then to today's Department of Energy. What has changed since the end of the cold war (boosted by 9/11) are three things. First, the flow of information has altered fundamentally, from paper to the Internet, making the control of information vastly more difficult, allowing data to be distributed, searched, and mined in ways unimaginable in the paper world. Second, the Manichaean twin worlds of the cold war have been shattered. Gone are the days when nuclear submarines faced nuclear submarines, fighter jets faced fighter jets, and tanks rumbled against other tanks. And third, administration fears in the early twenty-first century fastens on sub- or supra-national groups. And these entities have no particular interest in the latest, greatest technology: a clunky 1945 A-bomb wasn't the heart's desire of the Soviet Union in its last years. For a terrorist, an antique nuke is altogether as serviceable as the last one off the assembly line. All this has ushered in a new kind of terror-driven secrecy, one in which those creating secrets have come to think of everything as potentially secret—not just advanced technology, but also dams and electric power plants, bridges and tunnels, malls and museums, old works and documents as well as recent ones. Plans for such infrastructure hadn't been hidden away during the Cold War—increasingly they are. Everything, everywhere is always a target. This is an epochal change in the remit of secrecy.

Current technologies such as "dataveillance" echo your notion of omnipresent suspicion. Where do you locate the technologies of today and what power, or threat, do they pose?

PG: A second aspect of secrecy has emerged, as you suggest, from "dataveillance." Data about travel, housing, money, web-surfing—all this

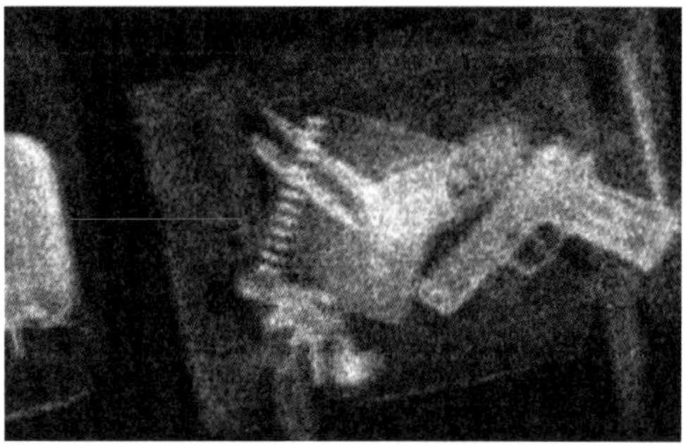

Stills from *Secrecy*, 2008

becomes a resource to be mined. Who will watch the watchers in the years to come? Will the Foreign Intelligence Surveillance Act (FISA) court do it? Will the legislature's intelligence oversight committee step up? Sometimes people protest that the courts, for example, can't deal with such secrets. Nonsense. Courts deal with secrets all the time, secrets of sexual assaults, secrets of crimes by minors, secrets of intellectual property, secrets of ongoing investigations. My own sense is that it is a losing proposition to try to define once and forever what kind of "dataveillance" is legitimate and what not. Ordinary surveillance was complicated enough when regulating something like the search of a car or home. That's why we had better have watchers watching the watchers; without serious, tough-minded oversight, our underlying democratic institutions are in deep trouble.

We were struck by the incorporation of artists in your film, especially because Jenny Holzer and Ben Rubin are participants in For Reasons of State. *Can you expand upon your choice of these two artists?*

PG: Information is both invisible and powerful, so right away, the shared problem of writing, filming, or making artworks about it becomes front and central. Make that secret information and the problem enters twice—hidden invisibility. In making the film, Robb and I liked this impossible challenge of picturing what by nature and design could not be seen. Our choices were guided by this: framing interview subjects with allusive rear-projected images, using light and dark on the set, depicting documents moving in and out of darkness, passing from film to Ruth Lingford's remarkable black-and-white woodcut- styled animation. We chose these artists (Jenny Holzer, Ben Rubin, Mark Hansen, and Jim Sanborn) because they contributed to this ethos, this borderland between hard-boiled analytic politics and the imaginary world. What I like about Holzer's piece, *For the City* (2005), in which she projected declassified documents from the post-9/11 moment, is that it embraces these contradictory pulls: secret documents . . . and yet released, redacted; documents that were hidden . . . now blown up to the size of the New York University Library viewed by all who passed by just south of Washington Square Park.

RM: The scale of Holzer's work makes monumental and public what was once diminished and bureaucratic. While clearly selected for the irony, I loved that the building she chose to project upon was a library; when we started *Secrecy* we thought we might like to make a film in which a librarian would figure in some heroic way. Likewise, Listening Post (2000–06), by Ben Rubin and Mark Hansen, manages to represent the inhuman scale and human intimacy that flows through the Internet at any given moment. The work sends one's mind reeling as they found ways to get their arms around the enormity and specificity of the web, and, for our purpose, helped make visceral that part of our film, which wants to move us from cold war notions of information control into this post-cold war age of information dissemination. Their work, so beautifully achieved, also gave us inspiration to continue in our work.

Your exploration of secrecy in today's administration carries on this residue of cold war politics-secrecy both protects and destroys the safety of today's public. With your presentation of both sides of the argument, what are the gains of a more objective methodology?

PG: To me "balance," a little of this versus a little of that, is in and of itself useless: add plus twenty-three to minus twenty-three and you get zero. But a position presented in isolation from alternatives is less than zero; it is tedious agitprop that dissolves into nothing at all, boring the converted and alienating those not already true believers. I want to understand, to feel the force field of stances in the world that are *not* mine.

In light of today's current events—the erased CIA tapes as well as the potential grant of retroactive immunity to telecommunications companies that aided the Bush administration without warrant—can you speak about how secrecy and current legislation threatens our civilian liberties?

PG: To me the greatest threat is that we, collectively, stop thinking about secrecy as a sometimes necessary measure that *always* comes with costs. And those costs are many. There's the danger that secrecy can abet or encourage bad actions, the danger that secrecy blocks the other branches of government from acting positively, and the danger that it isolates the public from deliberating basic decisions such as the decision to go to war. My greatest fear is that we can come to believe that that our civil liberties are totems that, once sacrificed, will make us safer for having given them up.

This brings me to one last point. Sometimes we speak as if politics is—or should be—a purely analytical affair. When someone says, "that is just political theater," the suggestion seems to be that *real* politics *isn't* performative, that aesthetics is the unnatural spin on something basic and pure. Conversely, for decades politics has often been treated as the unwanted intruder into the sacred fields of art; despite the myriad examples to the contrary, political art often becomes an epithet, socialist realism, version ten. I don't buy that dichotomy for a nanosecond. In the case of secrecy, making the dynamics of secrecy visible to where we can discuss it is already a form of politics. Sure, partisan maneuvering can be important, but what really interests me is real politics—the politics that lie at the possibility and limits of democratic deliberation.

PUBLIC DATABASE-BUREAUIT.ORG/ANTITERROR

ANTITERRORLINE

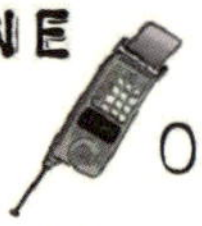

0000

US 1 212 998 3394

UK 0 207 987 0655

UPLOAD AN AUDIO REPORT

PRESS 1 FOR ANTITERROR

WORKS IN THE EXHIBITION

Bik Van der Pol
The Disappearance Piece, 1998
Stacks of publications
Dimensions variable
Collection of the artist

The Bureau of Inverse Technology
(Agents Natalie Jermijenko and Kate Rich)
Bit Plane, 1999
Single-channel video, black-and-white, sound;
13 minutes
Dimensions variable
Collection of the artist

Anti-terror Line, 2004-08
Audio Recording, speakers, and cards
Dimensions variable
Collection of the artist

Jenny Holzer
Final Autopsy Report DOD 13289 - DOD 13296 OCHRE, 2006
Oil on linen diptych
33 x 25.5 in. each
Courtesy Cheim & Read, New York

Small FORMICA 2851 YELLOW WHITE, 2006
Oil on linen
33 x 25.5 in.
Collection of the artist

Small FORMICA 2853 YELLOW WHITE, 2006
Oil on linen
33 x 25.5 in.
Collection of the artist

Lin + Lam
Unidentified Vietnam No. 29 from *Unidentified Vietnam*, 2006
Wood face plates, drawers, card catalogue cards, CD player, parabolic speaker, and signage stand
Dimensions variable
Collection of the artist

Pupils of Democracy from *Unidentified Vietnam*, 2006
Table, books, magnifying glass, 16mm film projector, film looper, projection screen, and 16mm film;
4 minutes
Dimensions variable
Collection of the artist

Mark Lombardi
Neil Bush, Silverado, MDC (2nd version), 1996
Graphite on paper
22 x 30 in.
Collection of Susan Swenson and Joe Amrhein

Trevor Paglen
Unmarked 737 at 'Gold Coast' Terminal/Las Vegas, NV/Distance ~1 mile/10:44 pm, 2005
Chromogenic color print
30 x 36 in.
Courtesy Bellwether Gallery, New York

The Salt Pit, Northeast of Kabul, Afghanistan, 2006
Chromogenic color print
24 x 36 in.
Courtesy Bellwether Gallery, New York

Illuminated Hangars/Tonopah Test Range, NV/Distance ~18 miles/9:08 pm, 2005
Chromogenic color print
30 x 36 in.
Courtesy Bellwether Gallery, New York

Ben Rubin
Dark Source, 2005
Microfiche monitors and ink on paper
Dimensions variable
Collection of the artist

Susan Schuppli
Stretch, 2007-08
Nine digital prints and single-channel video, color, sound; 4½ minutes
Dimensions variable
Collection of the artist

Speculative Archive
(Julia Meltzer and David Thorne)
"It's not my memory of it": three recollected documents, 2003
Single channel video, color, sound; 25 minutes
Dimensions variable

Photography credits: The copyright holders, photographers, and sources of visual material other than those indicated in the captions or checklist are as follows: frontispiece, pp. 4, 6, courtesy Pierogi Gallery; contents page, pp. 2, 34, 37, 38, courtesy Redacted Pictures; pp. 7, 8, courtesy Bellwether Gallery; pp. 26, 28, © Jenny Holzer/Artists Rights Society (ARS), New York; p. 29, courtesy Cheim & Read.

ACKNOWLEDGMENTS

The exhibition *For Reasons of State* and this catalogue would not have been possible without the care of many colleagues, friends, and advisers. The Independent Study Program is supported in part by Joanne Leonhardt Cassullo, The Dorothea L. Leonhardt Foundation, Inc.; the Dorothea L. Leonhardt Fund of the Communities Foundation of Texas, Inc.; The Edward and Sally Van Lier Fund of the New York Community Trust; the Easton Foundation; and the Whitney Contemporaries of the Whitney Museum of American Art. Endowment support is provided by the Communities Foundation of Texas, Inc.; The Dorothea L. Leonhardt Foundation, Inc.; the Helena Rubinstein Foundation; and George S. Harris. We extend our gratitude to Jennifer Gonzalez, 2007-08 Joanne Leonhardt Cassullo Fellow, for generous intellectual inspiration and for her commitment and support; and to Ron Clark, director of the Whitney Museum of American Art Independent Study Program, for his thoughtful guidance, conversations, and faith in the exhibition. Thanks are also due to Eva Diaz, former instructor for curatorial studies, and Sarah Lookofsky, program administrator, for their continuous efforts, advice, and support. We are grateful to our colleagues in the Independent Study Program, whose suggestions and concerns were invaluable in the conceptualization and construction of the exhibition. We would like to thank designer Sarah Vogwill for her patience and resourcefulness. At the Kitchen, we would like to acknowledge Debra Singer, Matthew Lyons, Nomaduma Masilela, and Stefan Jacobs for their guidance and coordination. Discussions with Gregg Bordowitz, Benjamin Buchloh, Mary Kelly, and Chantal Mouffe shaped our ideas in the early stages of exhibition planning. At the Whitney, our deep gratitude extends to Adam D. Weinberg, Alice Pratt Brown Director, and several in the curatorial department—Donna De Salvo, Carter Foster, Chrissie Iles, Shamim Momim, Christiane Paul, and Elisabeth Sussman—whose counsel proved to be essential in shaping our exhibition. We would also like to thank Beth Huseman, editor, for her helpful suggestions and other Whitney staff members, including Hillary de Marchena, Carol Rusk, Barbi Spieler, and Rachel de W. Wixom. The development of *For Reasons of State* is due in large part to the generous assistance of many individuals outside the Museum. Special thanks to Avi Alpert, Karen Beckman, Daria Cercek, Gordon Cooke, Christopher Fleming, Peter Galison, Thomas Keenan, Adam Kleinman, Erin Lee, Simon Leung, Thomas Y. Levin, Yates McKee, Meleko Mokgosi, Robb Moss, Tyler Poniatowski, and the Flemish community. Of crucial importance are the galleries and collectors who loaned works to the exhibition. And, of course, it is to the artists featured in *For Reasons of State* that we owe our greatest appreciation.

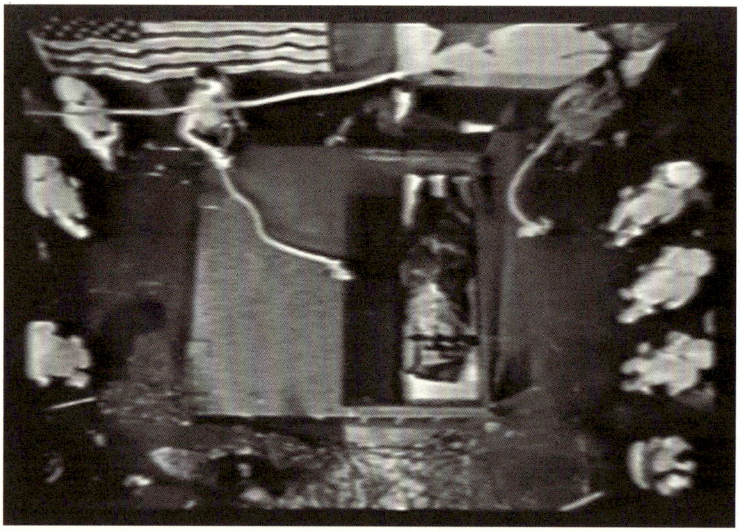